Supports
The Four-Blocks®
Literacy Model

# Big Words for Big Kids:
## Systematic Sequential Phonics
## and Spelling

by

Patricia M. Cunningham

Carson-Dellosa Publishing Company, Inc.
Greensboro, North Carolina

## Credits

**Editors:**
Joey Bland
Tracy Soles

**Cover Design:**
Matthew Van Zomeren

**Layout Design:**
Joey Bland

ISBN 0-88724-115-8

**Other Systematic Sequential Phonics and Spelling Books by Patricia M. Cunningham**

*Systematic Sequential Phonics They Use* (Carson-Dellosa, 2000)

*Prefixes and Suffixes: Systematic Sequential Phonics and Spelling* (Carson-Dellosa, 2002)

**Systematic Sequential Phonics and Spelling Word Card Sets**

Word Cards for Systematic Sequential Phonics (Carson-Dellosa, 2001)

Word Cards for Prefixes and Suffixes: Systematic Sequential Phonics and Spelling (Carson-Dellosa, 2002)

Big Words for Big Kids Word Card Set (Carson-Dellosa, 2003)

**Other Four-Blocks Books for Upper Grades**

*Month-by-Month Phonics for Upper Grades* by Patricia M. Cunningham and Dorothy P. Hall (Carson-Dellosa, 1998)

*Writing Mini-Lessons for Upper Grades: The Big-Blocks™ Approach* by Dorothy P. Hall, Patricia M. Cunningham, and Amanda B. Arens (Carson-Dellosa, 2003)

# Big Words for Big Kids
## Table of Contents

CD-2420 Big Words for Big Kids

# Big Words for Big Kids
# Table of Contents

# Introduction

Pick up any newspaper or magazine, read the first few sentences of any article, and notice the big words—words that have eight or more letters:

> The SAT (**Scholastic Aptitude** Test), **denounced** as biased and **ineffective** by many **consumers,** is still the **gatekeeper** in most **American** schools. College **admissions officers** often **downplay** the **significance** of the exam in the **application** process, but then brag about their schools' scores in **recruitment brochures**.

> **Historically**, as a strike **deadline approaches**, the labor **negotiators** go **underground** and stop talking to the media. Fear of having the talks **derailed** by leaks causes both sides to stop talking and keep **bargaining**.

The first thing that strikes you in looking at these big words is that they are the "meaning carrying" words. Without them, you wouldn't know very much. The second thing you notice is that these words are relatively low-frequency words. You could read many articles and pages in books before once again encountering **recruitment**, **historically**, and **derailed**.

Starting at about the fourth-grade level, most of what we read contains a high percentage of big, relatively unfamiliar, low-frequency words. Because these big words contain most of the meaning in sentences, we cannot comprehend what we read unless we can pronounce and access meaning for these words. All good readers are able to quickly pronounce and associate meaning with words they have rarely ever read before. How does this happen? How did you pronounce and make meaning for words such as **admissions**, **derailed**, and **underground** the first time you encountered them in your reading?

Linguists, who study how language works, tell us that in English, morphemes are the keys to unlocking the pronunciation, spelling, and meaning for big words. Morphemes are roots, prefixes, and suffixes which combine in a variety of ways to make up big words. The word **admission** is simply the word **admit**—with the spelling changes that always occur when **sion** is added to a word ending in **t**. The first time you saw **admissions**, your brain probably accessed similar words such as **permission**, **omission**, and **emission**. Using these other similar words, you quickly pronounced **admission**. Since you were probably aware that when you **permit** something, you give your **permission**, when you **omit** something, you have an **omission**, and the fumes that your car **emits** are called **emissions**. You probably also recognized the relationship between the word you had read many times—**admit**—and this new word **admissions**. Similarly, pronouncing and making meaning for **derailed** was not difficult if your brain thought of similar words such as **deported** and **declassified. Underground** is a compound word—its pronunciation and meaning are obvious by thinking of the pronunciation and meaning of the two root words, **under** and **ground**.

Morphemes—roots, prefixes, and suffixes—are the keys to unlocking the pronunciation, spelling, and meaning for big words. When you see a big word you have never encountered before in your reading, your brain thinks of similar big words and uses the understanding it has about how these big words work to quickly pronounce and access meaning for the new word. But what if your brain doesn't have very many big words stored there? What if you know some big words, but you have never realized how they were related to your smaller words? The lack of big words they can quickly access and associate meaning for renders many children from fourth grade up helpless when they encounter new big words.

According to the *Oxford English Dictionary*, a wimp is a "timid or ineffectual person." When you "wimp out," you withdraw from or avoid an undertaking. I spent time with this dictionary over the months in which I created *Big Words for Big Kids*. I learned new meanings for old words, discovered new words, and spent a lot of time pondering the derivations and histories of words. I came across this definition of "wimp" while searching for something else and was immediately struck with the image of many of the "big kids" I had taught. These big kids—mostly boys—were fearless about many things that terrified me, but they were terrified of any word with more than eight letters. Just the sight of one of these big words could cause one of my "almost-men boys" to put down the book and "give up without a fight." I even coined a word for this fear—morphophobia! Morphemes are the prefixes, suffixes, and roots—the meaningful chunks—which make up most big words. Many of the preteens I taught suffered from morphophobia—the irrational fear and dread of big words.

At the time, I determined that many of my students, even many of my average readers, suffered from morphophobia. The terms "wimp" and "wimp out" did not exist, or, at least, I was not aware of them. But when I chanced to read the definitions of wimp—while on my way to find a precise definition of wizard—I knew immediately that when it came to big words, my big kids were wimps. Not normally timid or ineffectual, they were when it came to big words, and they wimped out—skipped right over the word or fled the scene!

A wizard, according to my dictionary, is a person noted for his or her remarkable powers or exceptional ability within a certain sphere. Word wizards have remarkable powers and exceptional abilities to analyze words. As I pondered these definitions of wimps and wizards, I realized my real purpose in writing this book—to turn word wimps into word wizards. When encountering a new big word, word wizards do not "wimp out" and skip over the word, hoping no one will notice. Word wizards can pronounce, spell, and figure out a probable meaning for new big words, all through the magic of morphemes—prefixes, suffixes, and roots!

## The Lessons

*Big Words for Big Kids* contains 100 lessons which teach 33 common roots and all of the common prefixes and suffixes. The lessons are arranged in five-lesson cycles. The first four lessons in each cycle are Making Words lessons. The secret word that ends each Making Words lesson is a key word for one of the roots and contains at least one prefix or suffix. The fifth lesson in each cycle is a Word Wall lesson in which five words are added to the Word Wall. These words become the key words for using roots, prefixes, and suffixes to pronounce, spell, and get meaning for big words.

Following the 100 lessons are some Review and Extension Activities. These can be used for additional practice as the lessons are being done, as well as when all of the lessons are completed. In addition to providing practice with the Word Wall words, these activities extend the instruction so that students see how the prefixes and suffixes they have learned can help them read and spell hundreds of other words.

# The Scope and Sequence

The early lessons work with familiar English root words, such as **bright**, **power**, **weigh**, **act**, and **please**. Each root word is combined with common prefixes and suffixes to form big words. At least two examples for every root word become key words on the Word Wall.

Here is the list of the common root words taught in this book and the key word examples.

| Root Word | Key Words |
|---|---|
| **bright** | brighten  brightest  brightness |
| **magnet** | magnetic  demagnetize |
| **power** | powerful  powerfully  powerless |
| **weigh** | overweight  underweight |
| **create** | creatures  creator  recreation |
| **please** | pleasures  displeased |
| **act** | actors  actresses  reactions  interactive  transaction |
| **cover** | discovery  uncovered  undercover |
| **appear** | reappeared  disappearance |
| **courage** | encouraging  encouragement  discouraged  courageous  courageously |
| **sign** | signature  resignation  assignment  significant  insignificant |
| **place** | irreplaceable  misplaced |
| **lead** | misleading  leadership |
| **depend** | independent  independence |
| **nation** | national  international  nationalities |
| **health** | healthier  unhealthiest |
| **class** | classic  declassify  classification |
| **press** | depressing  expression  repress  unimpressive  pressurized |
| **form** | performance  reformed  deformity  formal  formulates |

As the lessons continue, some roots that are not familiar English words are taught. These roots are the most common Latin roots, and students learn how the meanings of these roots combine with prefixes and suffixes to create big words. Here is a list of the Latin roots taught in this book, their common meanings, and the key words added to the Word Wall.

| Root | Meaning | Key Words |
|------|---------|-----------|
| **port** | carry/bring | reporters  importance  transportation  portable  exportable |
| **dic** | say/speak | predictions  unpredictable  contradictions  dictator  dictatorship |
| **mis/mit** | send | permission  transmitted  emission |
| **pos** | put/place | composers  impossibility |
| **ven** | come | prevention  intervention  inventor |
| **spec** | look/watch | inspectors  spectators |
| **vis** | see | television  supervision |
| **tract** | drag/pull | subtraction  retraction  tractor |
| **jec** | throw | projectors  inject |
| **spir** | breathe | inspired  uninspired  conspirators |
| **fec** | make/do | infectious  perfectly  imperfectly |
| **struct** | build | construction  indestructible |
| **bio** | life | biologists  bionic  antibiotics |
| **cred** | believe/trust | incredible  creditors |

The words added to the word wall as key words are the most familiar words, and in most cases, these words, such as **inspired**, **construction**, and **subtraction**, will be in the listening/speaking vocabularies of your students. Once students learn to spell these key words and understand the relationships between the roots, prefixes, and suffixes, they will be able to use these known words to pronounce and access meaning for similar words. A few words—**displaced**, **deformity**, **transmitted**, **supervision**, **infectious**, **creditors, etc.**—may not be in your students' hearing/speaking vocabularies. These words were needed in order for the 100 Word Wall key words to contain at least two examples for every root and one example for every common prefix and suffix. You may need to build meaning for these words so that they, too, can become useful key words in your students' word stores.

# Prefixes

Prefixes are parts added to the beginnings of words that change the meanings of words. In English, four prefixes—**un**, **re**, **dis**, and **in**—account for over half the prefixed words. Because they are so common and their meaning change is so consistent, most children learn to recognize and use these prefixes. Other prefixes are less common, but have a consistent and predictable meaning. **Over**, **under**, **sub**, **super**, and **anti** are examples of prefixes which don't begin many words, but which should be taught because their meaning is obvious and consistent. There are some prefixes for which the meaning is not obvious to most students. Once they learn, however, that **mis** means "bad" or "wrong," that **inter** means "between or among," that **pre** means "before," and that **tele** means "far or distant," then they can use these meanings to build meaning for big words containing these prefixes. The most difficult group of prefixes have meanings that are difficult to explain and often change their spelling depending on the letters that follow. **Ex**, for example, means "out" but changes to **e** in words like **emission**. **Ad** means "toward" but often becomes **a** and the first letter of the root word as in **assignment**. **Ob** means "against" as in **objections**, but like **ad**, it often occurs as **o** with the first letter of the root word as in **oppress**. The meanings of prefixes like **per** and **com/con** are often not obvious and sometimes difficult to explain. These prefixes may not be helpful in providing meaning for a word, but they are still useful pronunciation chunks.

Here is a list of the prefixes, their common meanings, and key words taught in *Big Words for Big Kids*. Students should be able to use all of them as pronunciation keys, and some of them as clues to the meanings of big words.

| Prefix and Common Meaning | Word Wall Word |
| --- | --- |
| **a/ad** (**to**, **toward**) | assignment |
| **anti** (**against**) | antibiotics |
| **com/con** (**with**, **together**) | composers  conspirators  construction |
| **contra** (**against**) | contradictions |
| **de** (**opposite**, **down**) | demagnetizer declassify  deformity  depressing indestructible |
| **dis** (**not**, **do the opposite**) | displeased  discovery  disappearance  discouraged |
| **en** (**make**) | encouraging  encouragement |
| **e/ex** (**out**) | emission  expression  exportable |
| **im/in** (**in**) | unimpressive  importance  inspectors  inventor uninspired  inject  infectious |
| **im/in/ir** (**not**) | impossibility  imperfectly  independence  independent insignificant  incredible  indestructible  irreplaceable |
| **inter** (**between**, **among**) | interactive  international  intervention |
| **mis** (**wrong**, **badly**) | misplaced  misleading |
| **ob** (**against**) | objections |
| **per** (**through**) | performance  permission  perfectly  imperfectly |
| **pre** (**before**, **earlier**) | predictions  unpredictable  prevention |

| Prefix and Common Meaning | Word Wall Word |
|---|---|
| **pro** (**for**, **forward**) | projectors |
| **re** (**back**, **again**) | reactions  resignation  recreation  reappeared  reformed  retraction  irreplaceable  repress  reporters |
| **sub** (**under**, **less**) | subtraction |
| **super** (**beyond**, **more**) | supervision |
| **tele** (**far**) | television |
| **trans** (**across**) | transaction  transportation  transmitted |
| **un** (**not**, **opposite**) | unhealthiest  unimpressive  unpredictable  uninspired  uncovered |
| **over** (**over**, **beyond**) | overweight |
| **under** (**under**, **beneath**) | underweight  undercover |

## Suffixes

Suffixes are parts added to the ends of words that change how the words can be used in sentences and sometimes change or add meaning. Some suffixes are fairly easy to explain. Adding **er** or **est** to words adds the meaning of "more" or "most." The suffixes **en**, **ize**, **ify**, and **ate** often mean to make a certain way. You make a room **bright** when you **brighten** it. You make an airplane have **pressure** when you **pressurize** it. When you **classify** things, you put them into different **classes**. When you make things according to a **formula**, you **formulate** them. **Less**, **ful**, and **able/ible** are very consistent and easy to understand. Someone that is **powerless** has no **power**, and someone who is **powerful** has much **power**. Things that cannot be **predicted** are **unpredictable**, and things that cannot be **destroyed** are **indestructible**. When **ly** is added to words, it adds "in that way" meaning. If you do something **powerfully**, you do it in a **powerful** way. The suffixes **er** and **or** often indicate a person or thing that does something. **Reporters report**, and **inventors invent**. The suffix **ist** often indicates a person, and the suffix **ess** often indicates a female person. **Biologists** do **biology**, and **actresses act**. Some suffixes affect how a word can be used grammatically. **Tion/sion**, **ance/ence**, **ment**, **ness**, **y**, and **ture/sure** are often added to verbs to turn them into nouns. **Al**, **ous**, and **ic** often signal adjectives. We don't want to overemphasize grammar when teaching suffixes because grammar does not seem to play any role in what your brain does to pronounce and get meaning for an unfamiliar word. When you first saw the word **admission**, your brain did not think, "That word ends in **sion**. It must have been a verb that is turned into a noun! What verb could it have been?"

Rather, your brain accessed other **sion** words and the root words they went with (**permit/permission**; **omit/omission**; **emit/emission**) and used these as key words to pronounce and associate meaning for **admission**. In teaching our students about these suffixes, we try to avoid a lot of grammatical jargon. We do point out that some suffixes change doing words (verbs) into naming words (nouns), but we keep our emphasis on how the words are related and the consistency of that relationship. It is a lot more important for students to be able to verbalize that **reactions** are what you do when you **react**, and **creatures** are things you **create**, than for them to be able to name the part of speech.

Here are the suffixes, meanings, and key words taught in *Big Words for Big Kids*.

| Suffix and Possible Meaning | Word Wall Word |
|---|---|
| **er/est (more/most)** | brightest  healthier  unhealthiest |
| **en (to make)** | brighten |
| **ize (to make)** | demagnetize  pressurized |
| **ify (y changes to i) (to make)** | declassify  classification |
| **ate (to make)** | formulates |
| **less (without)** | powerless |
| **ful (full of/having)** | powerful  powerfully |
| **able/ible (able to be)** | irreplaceable  portable  exportable  unpredictable  indestructible  incredible |
| **ly (in that way)** | powerfully  courageously  perfectly  imperfectly |
| **er/or (person or thing that. . .)** | reporters  composers  leadership  dealership  actors  creator  dictator  dictatorship  spectators  inventor  inspectors  tractor  conspirators  projectors  creditors |
| **ist (person)** | biologists |
| **ess (female person)** | actresses |
| **tion/sion (nouns from verbs)** | recreation  transportation  classification  resignation  reactions  transaction  predictions  contradictions  intervention  retraction  subtraction  prevention  distraction  construction  expression  emission  permission  television  supervision |
| **ance/ence (nouns from verbs)** | importance  performance  disappearance  independence |
| **ment (nouns from verbs)** | encouragement  assignment |
| **ness (nouns)** | brightness |
| **y/ity (y changes to i) (nouns)** | discovery  deformity  impossibility  nationalities |
| **sure/ture (nouns)** | pleasures  pressurized  creatures  signature |
| **ant/ent (adjectives/describing words)** | significant  insignificant  independent |
| **al (adjectives)** | formal  national  international  nationalities |
| **ive (adjectives)** | interactive  unimpressive |
| **ous (adjectives)** | courageous  courageously  infectious |
| **ic (adjectives)** | magnetic  bionic |
| **ship (quality of)** | leadership  dealership  dictatorship |

CD-2420 Big Words for Big Kids

# Making Words Lessons

Making Words lessons are hands-on, minds-on manipulative activities through which students discover how the English spelling system works. Students are given letters and use these letters to make words as directed by the teacher or tutor. In *Big Words for Big Kids*, students are handed a letter strip containing all of the letters needed for the lesson. After writing the capital letters on the back, a student cuts the strip into letters and uses the letters to make words. (Reproducible letter strips are found on pages 172-191.) Students make 10-12 words in each lesson, including the secret word that uses all of the letters.

The words made in each lesson were carefully chosen so that every word has another related word in that same lesson. Once the 10-12 words are made, the Sort step of the lesson begins. The words are displayed on cards. Students read all of the words in the order made. They are then asked to sort the related words. Related words are words that share a common root word. As students sort the related words, they use these words in a sentence and explain how the words are related. Here are the words sorted from Lesson 43, in which the secret word is **international**:

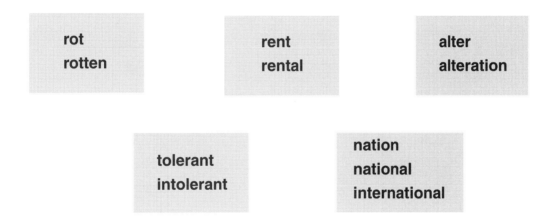

Students' explanations should focus on meaning and how the words are used in sentences:

"When something **rots**, we say it is **rotten**."

"When you **rent** a car, you have a **rental** car."

"When you **alter** something, that's an **alteration**."

"The opposite of **tolerant** is **intolerant**."

"Problems that the **nation** has are **national** problems. **International** means between many nations."

The final step of a Making Words lesson is the Transfer step. Students are asked to spell some words that are related in the same way as the sorted words In this lesson, they spell **hid/hidden**, **person/personal**, and **mission/intermission**.

Because students like to manipulate the letters and come up with their own words, we usually give them a take-home sheet with the same letters used in the lesson. (See p. 145 for a reproducible Making Words Take-Home Sheet.) The sheet has the letters across the top and blocks for writing words. Each student writes capital letters on the back and then cuts the letters apart. She manipulates the letters to make words and then writes them in the blocks. This is a popular homework assignment with students and their parents. When we write the letters at the top, we write them in alphabetical order—vowels, then consonants—so we don't give away the secret word. Students love being the "smart" ones who "know the secret word," watching parents and other relatives try to figure it out.

| Making Words Take-Home Sheet | | |
|---|---|---|
| a  a  e  i  i  o  l  n  n  n  r  t  t | | |
| | | |
| | | |
| | | |
| | | |
| | | |

CD-2420 Big Words for Big Kids     © Carson-Dellosa

# The Word Wall

The Word Wall is a critical component of *Big Words for Big Kids*. Five words are added to the Word Wall in every fifth lesson. These words provide key word examples for the roots, prefixes, and suffixes. Words are displayed on the wall under the letter of the alphabet with which they begin and in the order they are introduced in the lessons. (They are not alphabetized by the second letter, but are simply placed under the letter with which they begin.)

When words are added to the wall, we discuss the roots, prefixes, suffixes, and spelling changes. We chant the spelling of each word three times to provide an auditory/rhythmic route for retrieving the words. As we cheer for the words, we emphasize the morphemic parts—roots, prefixes, and suffixes—by pausing briefly and rhythmically before each part.

**"International, i-n-t-e-r—n-a-t-i-o-n—al!"**

The final activity helps students use the prefixes and suffixes in the new key words. The teacher says a sentence and the students decide on a related word which has one of the suffixes or prefixes and can complete the sentence.

A reproducible Take-Home Word Wall is given to students each time new words are added. This Take-Home Word Wall can also be used as the only word wall if an individual student is being tutored with this program. (Reproducible Take-Home Word Walls are found on pages 152-171.)

Because we want these Word Wall words to become the key words students can quickly access to help them pronounce, spell, and build meaning for other big words, students need lots of practice with them. Starting with Lesson 6, each Making Words lesson ends with a Be a Mind Reader Word Wall Review Activity which helps students become automatic at spelling these critical key words.

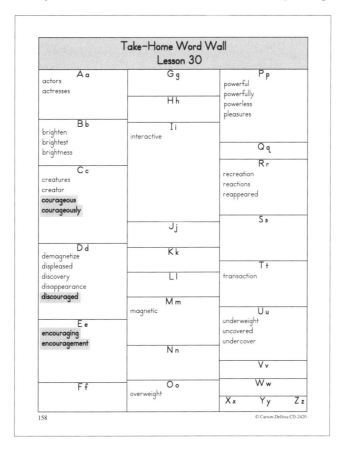

Here is the list of Word Wall words:

| | | |
|---|---|---|
| actors | formal | pressurized |
| actresses | formulates | prevention |
| antibiotics | healthier | projectors |
| assignment | imperfectly | reactions |
| biologists | importance | reappeared |
| bionic | impossibility | recreation |
| brighten | incredible | reformed |
| brightest | independence | reporters |
| brightness | independent | repress |
| classic | indestructible | resignation |
| classification | infectious | retraction |
| composers | inject | signature |
| conspirators | insignificant | significant |
| construction | inspectors | spectators |
| contradictions | interactive | subtraction |
| courageous | international | supervision |
| courageously | intervention | television |
| creator | inventor | tractor |
| creatures | irreplaceable | transaction |
| creditors | leadership | transmitted |
| dealership | magnetic | transportation |
| declassify | misleading | uncovered |
| deformity | misplaced | undercover |
| demagnetize | national | underweight |
| depressing | nationalities | unhealthiest |
| dictator | objections | unimpressive |
| dictatorship | overweight | uninspired |
| disappearance | perfectly | unpredictable |
| discouraged | performance | |
| discovery | permission | |
| displeased | pleasures | |
| emission | portable | |
| encouragement | powerful | |
| encouraging | powerfully | |
| exportable | powerless | |
| expression | predictions | |

CD-2420 Big Words for Big Kids

# Lesson 1

### Letters: e  i  b  g  h  r  s  t  t
**Words:** hit  sit  bit  bite  hits  tight  right  rights  bright  sitter  tighter  brightest

**Make Words:** Distribute the letters and tell students what words to make. After each word is made, show the correct spelling. Make sure everyone has each word spelled correctly before doing the next word. Keep the lesson fast paced.

1. Take 3 letters and spell **hit**. He **hit** the ball.
2. Change 1 letter and spell **sit**. I will **sit** on the sofa.
3. Change 1 letter and spell **bit**. The dog **bit** my hand.
4. Add 1 letter and spell **bite**. It was not a very bad **bite**.
5. Use 4 letters to spell **hits**. Our team got five **hits** in one inning.
6. Start over and use 5 letters to spell **tight**. Don't tie the rope too **tight**.
7. Change 1 letter and spell **right**. She got the **right** answer.
8. Add 1 letter and spell **rights**. They fought for their **rights**.
9. Start over and use 6 letters to spell **bright**. The sun is very **bright**.
10. Use 6 letters to spell **sitter**. I need to find a dog **sitter** for this weekend.
11. Use 7 letters to spell **tighter**. Pull the rope a little **tighter**.
12. Now it's time for the secret word. Take a minute to see if you can figure it out. (After 1 minute, give clues if needed.) Add 3 letters to a word you have already made and spell **brightest**. The sun shines **brightest** in July.

**Sort:** Display the words on cards in the order they were made, and have each word read aloud. Have the related words sorted. Talk with students about how the words are related, and have students make sentences that combine the related words.

| right | sit | hit | bright | tight | bit |
|---|---|---|---|---|---|
| rights | sitter | hits | brightest | tighter | bite |

**Transfer:** Have students use the related words to spell and make sentences for similar words:

tightest  brighter  hitter  light/lighter/lightest

# Lesson 2

## Letters: e i b g h n r s s t
## Words: be  sing  sting  being  tiger  tigers  bright  singers  stingers  brighten  brightness

**Make Words:** Distribute the letters and tell students what words to make. After each word is made, show the correct spelling. Make sure everyone has each word spelled correctly before doing the next word. Keep the lesson fast paced.

1.  Take 2 letters and spell **be**. <u>I will **be** back soon.</u>
2.  Take 4 letters and spell **sing**. <u>I **sing** in the choir.</u>
3.  Add 1 letter and spell **sting**. <u>A bee can **sting** you.</u>
4.  Use 5 letters to spell **being**. <u>They were just **being** silly.</u>
5.  Use 5 letters to spell **tiger**. <u>A **tiger** is a beautiful animal.</u>
6.  Add 1 letter to spell **tigers**. <u>**Tigers** live in jungles.</u>
7.  Use 6 letters to spell **bright**. <u>That light is too **bright**.</u>
8.  Use 7 letters to spell **singers**. <u>The choir had over 100 **singers**.</u>
9.  Add 1 letter to spell **stingers**. <u>Bees sting you with their **stingers**.</u>
10. Use 8 letters to spell **brighten**. <u>When the sun comes up, it will **brighten** the sky.</u>
11. Now it's time for the secret word. Take a minute to see if you can figure it out. (After 1 minute, give clues if needed.) Add 4 letters to a word you have already made and spell **brightness**. <u>We were amazed by the sun's **brightness** after three rainy days.</u>

**Sort:** Display the words on cards in the order they were made, and have each word read aloud. Have the related words sorted. Talk with students about how the words are related, and have students make sentences that combine the related words.

| be | sing | sting | tiger | bright |
|----|------|-------|-------|--------|
| being | singers | stingers | tigers | brighten |
| | | | | brightness |

**Transfer:** Have students use the related words to spell and make sentences for similar words:

tight/tightens/tightness  ring/ringers  go/going

# Lesson 3

### Letters: a  e  i  c  g  m  n  t
### Words: eat  act  mate  mean  meant  eating  acting  mating  inmate  magnet  magnetic

**Make Words:** Distribute the letters and tell students what words to make. After each word is made, show the correct spelling. Make sure everyone has each word spelled correctly before doing the next word. Keep the lesson fast paced.

1. Take 3 letters and spell **eat**. My dog loves to **eat**.
2. Use 3 letters to spell **act**. I will **act** in the play.
3. Take 4 letters and spell **mate**. He got a job as a **mate** on a ship.
4. Use 4 letters to spell **mean**. Did you **mean** to leave your book here?
5. Add a letter to spell **meant**. Yes, I **meant** to leave the book for you to read.
6. Use 6 letters to spell **eating**. The children are in the kitchen **eating** soup.
7. Use 6 letters to spell **acting**. He wants to get a job **acting** in a play.
8. Use 6 letters to spell **mating**. Spring is **mating** season for robins.
9. Use 6 letters to spell **inmate**. An **inmate** is someone who is in prison.
10. Use 6 letters to spell **magnet**. She used a **magnet** to attach her drawing to the refrigerator.
11. Now it's time for the secret word. Take a minute to see if you can figure it out. (After 1 minute, give clues if needed.) Add 2 letters to a word you have already made and spell **magnetic**. They used a **magnetic** compass.

**Sort:** Display the words on cards in the order they were made, and have each word read aloud. Have the related words sorted. Talk with students about how the words are related, and have students make sentences that combine the related words. Note the change in pronunciation in mean/meant.

| eat    | act    | mate   | mean   | magnet   |
|--------|--------|--------|--------|----------|
| eating | acting | mating | meant  | magnetic |
|        |        | inmate |        |          |

**Transfer:** Have students use the related words to spell and make sentences for similar words:

### playmate  skate/skating  treat/treating

# Lesson 4

### Letters: a e e e i d g m n t z
**Words: eat tame name named tamed eaten eating magnet detain detainee magnetize demagnetize**

**Make Words:** Distribute the letters and tell students what words to make. After each word is made, show the correct spelling. Make sure everyone has each word spelled correctly before doing the next word. Keep the lesson fast paced.

1.  Take 3 letters and spell **eat**. What time do we **eat**?
2.  Use 4 letters to spell **tame**. The squirrels in the park are very **tame**.
3.  Change 1 letter and spell **name**. What did you **name** the baby?
4.  Add a letter to spell **named**. We **named** the baby Alex.
5.  Change a letter to spell **tamed**. The trainer **tamed** the wild bear.
6.  Use 5 letters to spell **eaten**. The lost boy had not **eaten** in three days.
7.  Use 6 letters to spell **eating**. He is **eating** a cheeseburger and fries.
8.  Use 6 letters to spell **magnet**. A **magnet** attracts things made of iron or steel.
9.  Use 6 letters to spell **detain**. The police decided to **detain** the suspicious person.
10. Add 2 letters to spell **detainee**. We call someone who is detained a **detainee**.
11. Use 9 letters to spell **magnetize**. When you make something magnetic, you **magnetize** it.
12. Now it's time for the secret word. Take a minute to see if you can figure it out. (After 1 minute, give clues if needed.) Add 2 letters to **magnetize** and spell **demagnetize**. Our class did an experiment to see if we could demagnetize magnets.

**Sort:** Display the words on cards in the order they were made, and have each word read aloud. Have the related words sorted. Talk with students about how the words are related, and have students make sentences that combine the related words.

| | | | | |
|---|---|---|---|---|
| eat | name | magnet | tame | detain |
| eaten | named | magnetize | tamed | detainee |
| eating | | demagnetize | | |

**Transfer:** Have students use the related words to spell and make sentences for similar words:

beat/beaten/beating  equal/equalize  blame/blamed

# Lesson 5 Word Wall

**Word Wall Words: brighten  brightest  brightness  magnetic  demagnetize**

Give everyone a copy of the Take-Home Word Wall (p. 152) and/or place the words on the classroom Word Wall.

## Talk about the Words

Tell students that all of the Word Wall words are big words that began as smaller root words. Have students identify the two root words, **bright** and **magnet**. Explain to students that in English, many big words are smaller words with prefixes or suffixes added to them. Prefixes are parts added to the beginning of a word that change the meaning of the word. Suffixes are added to the end of words and change how that word can be used in a sentence. Discuss the prefixes, suffixes, and meaning changes for each word.

**brighten:** The root word is **bright** with the suffix **en**, which often means "to make." When you make something **bright**, you **brighten** it. When you make someone sad, you sadden them.

**brightest:** The root word is **bright** with the suffix **est**, which often makes a word mean "the most." The **brightest** star is the star that is the most **bright**. The prettiest flower is the flower that is the most pretty.

**brightness:** The root word is **bright** with the suffix **ness**. When we talk about something **bright**, we talk about its **brightness**. When we talk about someone who is happy, we talk about his happiness. The suffix **ness** often changes describing words (adjectives) to naming words (nouns).

**magnetic:** The root word is **magnet** with the suffix **ic**. When we talk about **magnets**, we say they are **magnetic**. When we talk about something done by a hero, we say it was heroic.

**demagnetize:** The root word is **magnet** with the prefix **de** and the suffix **ize**. The prefix **de** sometimes turns a word into its opposite. The opposite of **magnetize** is **demagnetize**. The opposite of increase is decrease. The suffix **ize** often means "to make something." When you magnetize something, you make it into a magnet. When you capitalize a word, you make the first letter into a capital.

## Cheer for the Words

Lead the class in cheering for each word in a rhythmic way, emphasizing the morphemic parts of the word "d-e—m-a-g-n-e-t—i-z-e." If possible, cheer for each new word three times.

## Use the Prefixes and Suffixes

Say these sentences aloud, and have students figure out a word with one of the prefixes or suffixes—**de**, **en**, **est**, **ness**, **ize**, **ic**—that will make sense in the sentence.

- I have a good **memory** so it is easy for me to _____ things.
- I was **sick** for a week, but now I have fully recovered from my _____.
- It has been a **hot** summer, but today was the _____ day yet.
- The president's papers were **classified**, but now they have been _____.
- I **hid** the present, but I forgot where it was _____.
- I'd like to be an **artist**, but probably won't because I'm not very _____.

# Lesson 6

**Letters:** e  e  o  l  p  r  s  s  w
**Words:** low  slow  rose  lose  loser  lower  power  roses  slower  powerless

**Make Words:** Distribute the letters and tell students what words to make. After each word is made, show the correct spelling. Make sure everyone has each word spelled correctly before doing the next word. Keep the lesson fast paced.

1. Take 3 letters and spell **low**. <u>The batter hit a **low** ball</u>.
2. Add 1 letter and spell **slow**. <u>We took a **slow** train to the game</u>.
3. Start over and use 4 letters to spell **rose**. <u>Everyone carried one red **rose**</u>.
4. Change 1 letter and spell **lose**. <u>No one thought we would **lose** the game</u>.
5. Add a letter to spell **loser**. <u>Unfortunately, every game has a winner and a **loser**</u>.
6. Change 1 letter to spell **lower**. <u>Our seats were on the **lower** deck</u>.
7. Change 1 letter and spell **power**. <u>Our new truck has a lot of **power**</u>.
8. Start over and use 5 letters to spell **roses**. <u>The bush is full of yellow **roses**</u>.
9. Use 6 letters to spell **slower**. <u>The opposite of faster is **slower**</u>.
10. Now it's time for the secret word. Take a minute to see if you can figure it out. (After 1 minute, give clues if needed.) Add four letters to a word you have already made and spell **powerless**. <u>The firefighters were **powerless** against the wind-driven flames</u>.

**Sort:** Display the words on cards in the order they were made, and have each word read aloud. Have the related words sorted. Talk with students about how the words are related, and have students make sentences that combine the related words. Point out the two uses of the suffix **er**—more and person.

| | | | | |
|---|---|---|---|---|
| **rose** | **low** | **slow** | **lose** | **power** |
| **roses** | **lower** | **slower** | **loser** | **powerless** |

**Transfer:** Have students use the related words to spell and make sentences for similar words:

**end/endless  help/helpless  worker  player  later  faster**

**Word Wall Review—Be a Mind Reader (p. 141)**

1. It's one of the words on the wall.
2. It does not have a prefix.
3. Magnet is not the root word.
4. It has more than 8 letters.
5. It ends with the suffix **ness**.

CD-2420 Big Words for Big Kids

# Lesson 7

## Letters: e  o  u  f  l  l  p  r  w  y
## Words: low  pull  full  fully  lowly  lower  power  fuller  pulley  powerful  powerfully

**Make Words:** Distribute the letters and tell students what words to make. After each word is made, show the correct spelling. Make sure everyone has each word spelled correctly before doing the next word. Keep the lesson fast paced.

1. Take 3 letters and spell **low**. He bumped his head on the **low** ceiling.
2. Take 4 letters and spell **pull**. My baby sister likes to **pull** my hair.
3. Change 1 letter and spell **full**. After the picnic, we were all **full**.
4. Add a letter and spell **fully**. The boat was **fully** equipped when we bought it.
5. Use 5 letters to spell **lowly**. He started out as a **lowly** private.
6. Use 5 letters to spell **lower**. **Lower** is the opposite of higher.
7. Change 1 letter to spell **power**. Our house is near a **power** plant.
8. Use 6 letters to spell **fuller**. My glass is **fuller** than yours.
9. Use 6 letters to spell **pulley**. They used a **pulley** to lift the heavy crate.
10. Use 8 letters to spell **powerful**. The town was hit by a **powerful** tornado.
11. Now it's time for the secret word. Take a minute to see if you can figure it out. (After 1 minute, give clues if needed.) Add 2 letters to **powerful** and spell **powerfully**. John Henry used his hammer **powerfully**.

**Sort:** Display the words on cards in the order they were made, and have each word read aloud. Have the related words sorted. Talk with students about how the words are related, and have students make sentences that combine the related words.

| | | | |
|---|---|---|---|
| full | low | pull | power |
| fully | lower | pulley | powerful |
| fuller | lowly | | powerfully |

**Transfer:** Have students use the related words to spell and make sentences for similar words:

slow/slower/slowly  quick/quicker/quickly  powerlessly

## Word Wall Review—Be a Mind Reader (p. 141)

1. It's one of the words on the wall.
2. It does not have a prefix.
3. It does not end with the suffix ness.
4. It has 8 letters.
5. It ends with the suffix **ic**.

# Lesson 8

**Letters:** e  e  i  o  g  h  r  t  v  w
**Words:** grow  grew  view  threw  throw  write  wrote  weigh  weight  growth  review overweight

**Make Words:** Distribute the letters and tell students what words to make. After each word is made, show the correct spelling. Make sure everyone has each word spelled correctly before doing the next word. Keep the lesson fast paced.

1. Take 4 letters and spell **grow**. I like to plant things and watch them **grow**.
2. Change 1 letter to spell **grew**. My little puppy **grew** into a huge dog.
3. Take 4 letters and spell **view**. Our room had a great **view** of the ocean.
4. Use 5 letters to spell **threw**. The pitcher **threw** the ball to first base.
5. Change 1 letter to spell **throw**. He can **throw** the ball very fast.
6. Use 5 letters to spell **write**. I like to **write** stories and poems.
7. Change 1 letter to spell **wrote**. I **wrote** a story about our trip to Disneyland.
8. Use 5 letters to spell **weigh**. How much do you **weigh**?
9. Add a letter to spell **weight**. I don't tell anyone my **weight**.
10. Use 6 letters to spell **growth**. We were amazed by the puppy's **growth**.
11. Use 6 letters to spell **review**. We are going to **review** everything before the test.
12. Now it's time for the secret word. Take a minute to see if you can figure it out. (After 1 minute, give clues if needed.) Add 4 letters to a word you have already made and spell **overweight**. The boxer was working out and dieting because he was a little **overweight**.

**Sort:** Display the words on cards in the order they were made, and have each word read aloud. Have the related words sorted. Talk with students about how the words are related, and have students make sentences that combine the related words. Note the change in spelling when throw, write, and grow are used in the past—threw, wrote, and grew.

| throw | write | grow | view | weigh |
|-------|-------|------|------|-------|
| threw | wrote | grew | review | weight |
| | | growth | | overweight |

**Transfer:** Have students use the related words to spell and make sentences for similar words:

draw/drew  fly/flew  overthrow  overview

## Word Wall Review—Be a Mind Reader (p. 141)

1. It's one of the words on the wall.
2. It does not end with the suffix ize.
3. Magnet is not the root word.
4. It has more than 8 letters.
5. It means **the most bright**.

# Lesson 9

### Letters: e  e  i  u  d  g  h  n  r  t  w
**Words:** diet  tied  untie  unite  united  untied  retied  dieter  weight  weighed  **reunite**
**underweight**

**Make Words:** Distribute the letters and tell students what words to make. After each word is made, show the correct spelling. Make sure everyone has each word spelled correctly before doing the next word. Keep the lesson fast paced.

1. Take 4 letters and spell **diet**. <u>I am on a **diet**</u>.
2. Move the letters in diet to spell **tied**. <u>She **tied** her brother's shoe</u>.
3. Use 5 letters to spell **untie**. <u>Please help me **untie** this shoe</u>.
4. Move the letters in untie to spell **unite**. <u>We must all **unite** if we are going to win this war</u>.
5. Add a letter to spell **united**. <u>Our country is totally **united**</u>.
6. Move the letters in united to spell **untied**. <u>His shoe was **untied**</u>.
7. Use 6 letters to spell **retied**. <u>He **retied** his shoe</u>.
8. Use the letters in retied to spell **dieter**. <u>A person on a diet is a **dieter**</u>.
9. Use 6 letters to spell **weight**. <u>His **weight** is 67 pounds</u>.
10. Use 7 letters to spell **weighed**. <u>I get **weighed** when I go to see the doctor</u>.
11. Use 7 letters to spell **reunite**. <u>After the disaster, the Red Cross worked to **reunite** children with their families</u>.
12. Now it's time for the secret word. Take a minute to see if you can figure it out. (After 1 minute, give clues if needed.) Add 5 letters to a word you have already made and spell **underweight**. <u>The boxer was bulking up because he was **underweight**</u>.

**Sort:** Display the words on cards in the order they were made, and have each word read aloud. Have the related words sorted. Talk with students about how the words are related, and have students make sentences that combine the related words.

| | | | |
|---|---|---|---|
| tied | unite | diet | weight |
| untie | united | dieter | weighed |
| untied | reunite | | underweight |
| retied | | | |

**Transfer:** Have students use the related words to spell and make sentences for similar words:

move/removed/unmoved   cover/recovered/uncovered   underline  underground

## Word Wall Review—Be a Mind Reader (p. 141)

1. It's one of the words on the wall.
2. It does not end with the suffix est.
3. It does not end with the suffix ness.
4. Bright is not the root word.
5. It means **the opposite of magnetize**.

# Lesson 10  Word Wall

**Word Wall Words: powerful  powerfully  powerless  overweight  underweight**

Give everyone a copy of the Take-Home Word Wall (p. 153) and/or place the words on the classroom Word Wall.

## Talk about the Words

Tell students that all of the Word Wall words are big words that began as smaller root words. Have students identify the two root words, **power** and **weight**. Remind students that in English, many big words are smaller words with prefixes or suffixes added to them. Prefixes are parts added to the beginning of the word that change the meaning of the word. Suffixes are added to the end of words and change how that word can be used in a sentence. Discuss the prefixes, suffixes, and meaning changes for each word.

**powerful:** The root word is **power** with the suffix **ful**, which often means "full of" or "having." When you have **power**, you are **powerful**. When something has beauty, it is beautiful.

**powerfully:** The root word is **power** with the suffixes **ful** and **ly**. **Ly** often signals that a word is an adverb. A person can be **powerful**, and she can do things **powerfully**. A person can be beautiful, and she can do things beautifully.

**powerless:** The root word is **power** with the suffix **less**, which often means "without" or "doesn't have." Words that end in **less** are often opposites of words that end in **ful**. A person who doesn't have any **power** is **powerless**. A person who has no money is penniless.

**overweight:** The root word is **weigh** with the prefix **over**, which often means "more," "over," or "too much." A person who is **overweight weighs** too much. A car that is overpriced costs too much.

**underweight:** The root word is **weight** with the prefix **under**, which often means "less," "under" or "not enough." A person who is **underweight** doesn't **weigh** enough. An underdog has less of a chance of winning.

## Cheer for the Words

Lead the class in cheering for each word in a rhythmic way, emphasizing the morphemic parts of the word "**p-o-w-e-r—f-u-l—l-y**." If possible, cheer for each new word three times.

## Use the Prefixes and Suffixes

Say these sentences aloud, and have students figure out a word with one of the prefixes or suffixes—**under**, **over**, **ful**, **less**, **ly**—that will make sense in the sentence.

- One word for what you **wear** under your clothes is _____.
- When something happens all of a **sudden**, we say it happened _____.
- I am always **forgetting** things, and my mom says I am _____.
- I **helped** my dad with the repairs, and he said I was very _____.
- My dog thinks everyone is her **friend**, and everyone says she is very _____.
- My dad worked a lot of extra **time** this week, but fortunately he gets paid for _____.
- I **hoped** to get an A on the test, but since the test was very hard, it seems _____.

*CD-2420 Big Words for Big Kids* © Carson-Dellosa

# Lesson 11

### Letters: a  e  e  u  c  r  r  s  t
**Words:** act  cute  cuter  cater  react  trace  rescue  rescuer  caterer  retrace  creates  creatures

**Make Words:** Distribute the letters and tell students what words to make. After each word is made, show the correct spelling. Make sure everyone has each word spelled correctly before doing the next word. Keep the lesson fast paced.

1. Take 3 letters and spell **act**. We were late and missed the first **act** of the play.
2. Use 4 letters to spell **cute**. What a **cute** puppy!
3. Add a letter to spell **cuter**. The other puppy is even **cuter**!
4. Change 1 letter and spell **cater**. My friend is going make food and **cater** the party.
5. Move the letters in cater to spell **react**. We had to **react** quickly when the alarm sounded.
6. Move the letters again to spell **trace**. **Trace** the pattern and then cut out the tree.
7. Use 6 letters and spell **rescue**. He works for the **rescue** squad.
8. Add a letter to spell **rescuer**. A person who rescues someone is called a **rescuer**.
9. Use 7 letters to spell **caterer**. The person who caters the meal is called the **caterer**.
10. Use 7 letters to spell **retrace**. This doesn't show up very well, so I am going to **retrace** it with a dark pen.
11. Use 7 letters to spell **creates**. She **creates** amazing sculptures.
12. Now it's time for the secret word. Take a minute to see if you can figure it out. (After 1 minute, give clues if needed.) The secret word ends with the suffix **tures**. Some of her sculptures are scary **creatures**.

**Sort:** Display the words on cards in the order they were made, and have each word read aloud. Have the related words sorted. Talk with students about how the words are related, and have students make sentences that combine the related words. Point out the two uses of the suffix **er**—more and person.

| act | trace | creates | cute | rescue | cater |
|-----|-------|---------|------|--------|-------|
| react | retrace | creatures | cuter | rescuer | caterer |

**Transfer:** Have students use the related words to spell and make sentences for similar words:

place/replace nice/nicer bake/baker rescuer

## Word Wall Review—Be a Mind Reader (p. 141)
1. It's one of the words on the wall.
2. It does not have a prefix.
3. Bright is not the root word.
4. It has 8 letters
5. It ends with the suffix **ful**.

# Lesson 12

## Letters: a e e i o c n r r t
## Words: act race racer react train create trainer trainee creator reaction recreation

**Make Words:** Distribute the letters and tell students what words to make. After each word is made, show the correct spelling. Make sure everyone has each word spelled correctly before doing the next word. Keep the lesson fast paced.

1. Take 3 letters and spell **act**. Sometimes he doesn't **act** right.
2. Take 4 letters and spell **race**. I won the **race**.
3. Add 1 letter and spell **racer**. I was the fastest **racer**.
4. Use 5 letters to spell **react**. She didn't know how to **react** to the news.
5. Use 5 letters to spell **train**. One of my mom's jobs is to **train** all of the new people.
6. Use 6 letters to spell **create**. I am going to **create** a huge mural.
7. Use 7 letters to spell **trainer**. The one who trains people is called the **trainer**.
8. Change 1 letter to spell **trainee**. The person being trained is the **trainee**.
9. Use 7 letters to spell **creator**. The person who creates something is the **creator**.
10. Use 8 letters to spell **reaction**. I could hardly wait to see his **reaction** when he got to the surprise party.
11. Now it's time for the secret word. Take a minute to see if you can figure it out. (After 1 minute, give clues if needed.) The secret word ends with the suffix **tion**. After school, we play basketball at the **recreation** center.

**Sort:** Display the words on cards in the order they were made, and have each word read aloud. Have the related words sorted. Talk with students about how the words are related, and have students make sentences that combine the related words. (When you do recreation, you are "recreating" yourself.)

| act | race | train | create |
|---|---|---|---|
| react | racer | trainer | creator |
| reaction | | trainee | recreation |

**Transfer:** Have students use the related words to spell and make sentences for similar words:

employ/employer/employee   action   creation

## Word Wall Review—Be a Mind Reader (p. 141)

1. It's one of the words on the wall.
2. It has more than 8 letters.
3. It has a prefix.
4. It does not have a suffix.
5. It begins with the prefix **over**.

# Lesson 13

### Letters: a e e u l p r s s
## Words: use sale seal reuse sleep asleep resale reseal sealer please pleasures

**Make Words:** Distribute the letters and tell students what words to make. After each word is made, show the correct spelling. Make sure everyone has each word spelled correctly before doing the next word. Keep the lesson fast paced.

1. Take 3 letters and spell **use**. What do you **use** this thing for?
2. Use 4 letters to spell **sale**. That house has a "For **sale**" sign.
3. Move the letters in sale to spell **seal**. Be sure and **seal** that bag after you use it.
4. Use 5 letters to spell **reuse**. I am going to save this jar and **reuse** it.
5. Use 5 letters to spell **sleep**. I **sleep** late on Saturdays.
6. Add a letter to spell **asleep**. I was fast **asleep** when the phone rang.
7. Use 6 letters to spell **resale**. When something has been sold before, we say it is up for **resale**.
8. Move the letters in resale to spell **reseal**. I had to **reseal** the envelope because I forgot to put the check in it.
9. Move the letters in reseal to spell **sealer**. Glue is a good **sealer**.
10. Use 6 letters to spell **please**. It will **please** me if you say you can come.
11. Now it's time for the secret word. Take a minute to see if you can figure it out. (After 1 minute, give clues if needed.) The secret word ends with the suffix **sures**. Taking a walk on the beach is one of life's greatest **pleasures**.

**Sort:** Display the words on cards in the order they were made, and have each word read aloud. Have the related words sorted. Talk with students about how the words are related, and have students make sentences that combine the related words.

| use | sale | seal | sleep | please |
|-----|------|------|-------|--------|
| reuse | resale | reseal | asleep | pleasures |
| | | sealer | | |

**Transfer:** Have students use the related words to spell and make sentences for similar words:

wake/awake   treasures   measures   play/replay/player

## Word Wall Review—Be a Mind Reader (p. 141)

1. It's one of the words on the wall.
2. It does not have the root word weight.
3. It does not have the root word bright.
4. It does have the root word **power**.
5. It does not have the suffix ful.

CD-2420 Big Words for Big Kids

## Lesson 14

### Letters: a  e  e  i  d  d  l  p  s  s

**Words:** leap  seal  pedal  sleep  asleep  leaped  sealed  please  pedaled  disease  diseased  displeased

**Make Words:** Distribute the letters and tell students what words to make. After each word is made, show the correct spelling. Make sure everyone has each word spelled correctly before doing the next word. Keep the lesson fast paced.

1. Take 4 letters and spell **leap**. These frogs can **leap** high and fast.
2. Use 4 letters to spell **seal**. The king put his **seal** on the paper.
3. Use 5 letters to spell **pedal**. Going downhill, I had to **pedal** really fast.
4. Use 5 letters to spell **sleep**. My brother and I **sleep** in the same room.
5. Add a letter to spell **asleep**. He is usually **asleep** before I am.
6. Use 6 letters to spell **leaped**. The frog **leaped** across the pond.
7. Use 6 letters to spell **sealed**. We **sealed** the envelope and mailed it.
8. Use 6 letters to spell **please**. I like my teacher and I try to **please** him.
9. Use 7 letters to spell **pedaled**. I **pedaled** hard to get up the hill.
10. Use 7 letters to spell **disease**. The man suffered from Parkinson's **disease**.
11. Add a letter to spell **diseased**. To save the herd, they had to kill the **diseased** cows.
12. Now it's time for the secret word. Take a minute to see if you can figure it out. (After 1 minute, give clues if needed.) Add 4 letters to a word you have already made and spell **displeased**. The teacher was very **displeased** when half the class forgot their homework.

**Sort:** Display the words on cards in the order they were made, and have each word read aloud. Have the related words sorted. Talk with students about how the words are related, and have students make sentences that combine the related words.

| leap | seal | pedal | sleep | disease | please |
|------|------|-------|-------|---------|--------|
| leaped | sealed | pedaled | asleep | diseased | displeased |

**Transfer:** Have students use the related words to spell and make sentences for similar words:

trust/trusted/distrusted   like/liked/disliked   prove/proved/disproved

### Word Wall Review—Be a Mind Reader (p. 141)

1. It's one of the words on the wall.
2. Magnet is not the root word.
3. Power is not the root word.
4. Bright is not the root word.
5. It begins with the prefix **under**.

# Lesson 15 Word Wall

## Word Wall Words: creatures  creator  recreation  pleasures  displeased

Give everyone a copy of the Take-Home Word Wall (p. 154) and/or place the words on the classroom Word Wall.

## Talk about the Words

Tell students that all of the Word Wall words are big words that began as smaller root words. Have students identify the two root words, **create** and **please**. Remind students that in English, many big words are smaller words with prefixes or suffixes added to them. Prefixes are parts added to the beginning of the word that change the meaning of the word. Suffixes are added to the end of words and change how that word can be used in a sentence. Discuss the prefixes, suffixes, and meaning changes for each word:

**creatures:** The root word is **create** with the suffix **ture** and the **s** ending. **Creatures** are things you **create**.

**creator:** The root word is **create** with the suffix **or**, which often signals a person or thing that does something. A **creator creates**. An actor acts. A donor donates.

**recreation:** The root word is **create** with the suffix **re** and the prefix **tion**. The **create/recreation** relationship is not obvious in this word. **Re** can signal "back" or "again." When you engage in **recreation**, you "recreate" yourself; you feel refreshed and create a "new you."

**pleasures:** The root word is **please** with the suffix **sure** and the **s** ending. Things that **please** you are **pleasures**.

**displeased:** The root word is **please** with the prefix **dis**, which often signals an opposite, and the **ed** ending. **Displeased** is the opposite of **pleased**. Distrust is the opposite of trust.

## Cheer for the Words

Lead the class in cheering for each word in a rhythmic way, emphasizing the morphemic parts of the word "r-e—c-r-e-a—t-i-o-n." If possible, cheer for each new word three times.

## Use the Prefixes and Suffixes

Say these sentences aloud, and have students figure out a word with one of the prefixes or suffixes—**ture**, **sure**, **or**, **re**, **tion**, **dis**—that will make sense in the sentence.

- A person who is not **honest** is _____.
- If you are **displeased** with something, your face will express your _____.
- The result of things that you **mix** together is called a _____.
- A person who **sails** a boat is a _____.
- Global positioning satellites know where you are **located** and can plot your exact _____.
- My Internet **connection** was broken, and I had to _____.

## Lesson 16

### Letters: a e e c r s s s t
### Words: act  eat  set  seat  react  reset  reseat  eaters  create  creates  actresses

**Make Words:** Distribute the letters and tell students what words to make. After each word is made, show the correct spelling. Make sure everyone has each word spelled correctly before doing the next word. Keep the lesson fast paced.

1. Take 3 letters and spell **act**. I like to **act** in plays.
2. Use 3 letters to spell **eat**. On a hot day, I like to **eat** ice cream.
3. Use 3 letters to spell **set**. He **set** the timer for 20 minutes.
4. Add 1 letter and spell **seat**. This is my **seat**.
5. Use 5 letters to spell **react**. I wondered how he would **react** when I told him the bad news.
6. Use 5 letters to spell **reset**. When the power came back on, we had to **reset** all of the clocks.
7. Add a letter and spell **reseat**. The usher told us we were in the wrong seats and she would have to **reseat** us.
8. Move the letters in reseat to spell **eaters**. My brothers are all big **eaters**.
9. Use 6 letters to spell **create**. I am going to **create** a masterpiece!
10. Add a letter to spell **creates**. He **creates** sculptures from junk.
11. Now it's time for the secret word. Take a minute to see if you can figure it out. (After 1 minute, give clues if needed.) Add your letters to a word you have already made and spell **actresses**. The actors and **actresses** all came out on stage for a final bow.

**Sort:** Display the words on cards in the order they were made, and have each word read aloud. Have the related words sorted. Talk with students about how the words are related, and have students make sentences that combine the related words.

| act | eat | set | seat | create |
|---|---|---|---|---|
| react | eaters | reset | reseat | creates |
| actresses | | | | |

**Transfer:** Have students use the related words to spell and make sentences for similar words:

play/replay  pay/repay  move/remove

**Word Wall Review—Be a Mind Reader (p. 141)**

1. It's one of the words on the wall.
2. It does not have a prefix.
3. Bright is not the root word.
4. **Create** is the root word.
5. It means **someone who creates something**.

# Lesson 17

### Letters: a e i o c n r s t
### Words: act nose race nice nicer react nicest nosier racist actors action reactions

**Make Words:** Distribute the letters and tell students what words to make. After each word is made, show the correct spelling. Make sure everyone has each word spelled correctly before doing the next word. Keep the lesson fast paced.

1. Take 3 letters and spell **act**. He is just putting on an **act**.
2. Take 4 letters and spell **nose**. The dog's **nose** was cold.
3. Use 4 letters to spell **race**. One of the questions on the form asked me for my **race**.
4. Use 4 letters to spell **nice**. Your mom is a very **nice** person.
5. Add a letter to spell **nicer**. I think your mom is **nicer** than Tammy's mom.
6. Use 5 letters to spell **react**. Firefighters have to **react** quickly when the alarm sounds.
7. Use 6 letters to spell **nicest**. We both have the **nicest** moms in the world!
8. Use 6 letters to spell **nosier**. My dog is **nosier** than your dog.
9. Use 6 letters to spell **racist**. A person who is prejudiced against a certain race is a **racist**.
10. Use 6 letters to spell **actors**. The **actors** in this play were very good.
11. Use 6 letters to spell **action**. The movie had lots of **action**.
12. Now it's time for the secret word. Take a minute to see if you can figure it out. (After 1 minute, give clues if needed.) Add letters to **action** to spell the secret word. Different people had different **reactions** to the news.

**Sort:** Display the words on cards in the order they were made, and have each word read aloud. Have the related words sorted. Talk with students about how the words are related, and have students make sentences that combine the related words.

| | | | |
|---|---|---|---|
| act | race | nice | nose |
| actors | racist | nicer | nosier |
| action | | nicest | |
| react | | | |
| reactions | | | |

**Transfer:** Have students use the related words to spell and make sentences for similar words:

organ/organist   motor/motorist   small/smaller/smallest

### Word Wall Review—Be a Mind Reader (p. 141)

1. It's one of the words on the wall.
2. It has 10 letters.
3. Create is not the root word.
4. It has a prefix.
5. **Please** is the root word.

# Lesson 18

## Letters: a e e i i c n r t t v
## Words: act train react create active trainee creative inactive interact interactive

**Make Words:** Distribute the letters and tell students what words to make. After each word is made, show the correct spelling. Make sure everyone has each word spelled correctly before doing the next word. Keep the lesson fast paced.

1. Take 3 letters and spell **act**. <u>**Act** your age!</u>
2. Use 5 letters to spell **train**. <u>I am trying to **train** my dog to do tricks.</u>
3. Use 5 letters to spell **react**. <u>The criminal didn't **react** as she read the verdict.</u>
4. Use 6 letters to spell **create**. <u>What are you going to **create**</u>?
5. Use 6 letters to spell **active**. <u>My dog is very **active**.</u>
6. Use 7 letters to spell **trainee**. <u>I was a **trainee** for two weeks on this new job.</u>
7. Use 8 letters to spell **creative**. <u>My sister is more **creative** than I am.</u>
8. Use 8 letters to spell **inactive**. <u>The opposite of active is **inactive**.</u>
9. Use 8 letters to spell **interact**. <u>I **interact** with my real friends at schools and with my virtual friends on the Internet.</u>
10. Now it's time for the secret word. Take a minute to see if you can figure it out. (After 1 minute, give clues if needed.) Add your letters to **interact** to spell the secret word. <u>I like computer games because they are **interactive**.</u>

**Sort:** Display the words on cards in the order they were made, and have each word read aloud. Have the related words sorted. Talk with students about how the words are related, and have students make sentences that combine the related words.

| | | |
|---|---|---|
| act | train | create |
| react | trainee | creative |
| active | | |
| inactive | | |
| interact | | |
| interactive | | |

**Transfer:** Have students use the related words to spell and make sentences for similar words:

invent/inventive    prevent/preventive    protect/protective

**Word Wall Review—Be a Mind Reader (p. 141)**

1. It's one of the words on the wall.
2. It does not have the root word weight.
3. It does not have the root word magnet.
4. It begins with a prefix.
5. It begins with the prefix **re**.

# Lesson 19

### Letters: a a i o c n n r s t t
### Words: act art artist action nation nations transact carnation carnations transaction

**Make Words:** Distribute the letters and tell students what words to make. After each word is made, show the correct spelling. Make sure everyone has each word spelled correctly before doing the next word. Keep the lesson fast paced.

1. Take 3 letters and spell **act**. When you get to the party, **act** surprised.
2. Change 1 letter to spell **art**. We took a field trip to the **art** museum.
3. Add 3 letters to spell **artist**. They had a special exhibit for my favorite **artist**.
4. Use 6 letters to spell **action**. My brother has lots of **action** figures.
5. Use 6 letters to spell **nation**. **Nation** is another word for country.
6. Add a letter to spell **nations**. The people at the meeting came from many **nations**.
7. Use 8 letters to spell **transact**. My dad travels because he has to **transact** business with stores all over the world.
8. Use 9 letters to spell **carnation**. Every person wore a red **carnation**.
9. Add a letter to spell **carnations**. **Carnations** are my favorite flowers.
10. Now it's time for the secret word. Take a minute to see if you can figure it out. (After 1 minute, give clues if needed.) Add your letters to a word you have already made and spell **transaction**. The business tycoon told the audience that he did his first business **transaction** when he was ten and sold his comic books to buy a bike.

**Sort:** Display the words on cards in the order they were made, and have each word read aloud. Have the related words sorted. Talk with students about how the words are related, and have students make sentences that combine the related words.

| art | act | carnation | nation |
|-----|-----|-----------|--------|
| artist | action | carnations | nations |
| | transact | | |
| | transaction | | |

**Transfer:** Have students use the related words to spell and make sentences for similar words:

invent/invention   subtract/subtraction   select/selection   collect/collection

## Word Wall Review—Be a Mind Reader (p. 141)

1. It's one of the words on the wall.
2. It has more than 8 letters.
3. It begins with a prefix.
4. It begins with the letter **d**.
5. It means **the opposite of pleased**.

# Lesson 20 Word Wall

**Word Wall Words: actors actresses reactions transaction interactive**

Give everyone a copy of the Take-Home Word Wall (p. 155) and/or place the words on the classroom Word Wall.

## Talk about the Words

Tell students that all of the Word Wall words today have the same root word, and have students determine that the root word is **act**. Have students pronounce each word and tell what has been added to **act**. Discuss how the prefixes and suffixes affect the meaning of the words.

**actors:** The root word is **act** with the suffix **or** and the **s** ending. **Actors** are people who **act**. In many words, the suffix **or** indicates the person or thing that does something.

**actresses:** The root word is **act** with the **es** ending and the suffix **ess**, which often signals a female person. An **actress acts**. A waitress waits on you. A hostess hosts the party.

**reactions:** The root word is **act** with the prefix **re,** the **s** ending, and the suffix **tion**. The prefix **re** often means "back" or "again." When you **react**, you **act** "back" in response to something that has happened. What you do or say as you **react** is called your **reaction**. What you create is your creation. **Tion** is often added to doing words (verbs), such as react, to turn them into naming words (nouns).

**transaction:** The root word is **act** with the prefix **trans** and the suffix **tion**. The prefix **trans** usually means "across" or "over." When you **transact** something, you usually make a deal. You hand something over to them, and they, in turn, usually hand something over to you. A transaction is what you have when you have transacted something.

**interactive:** The root word is **act** with the prefix **inter** and the suffix **ive**. The prefix **inter** means "between" or "among." When you **interact** with people, you do things, tell things, and share things among your group. The suffix **ive** is often added to doing words (verbs), such as interact, to turn them into describing words (adjectives). Something, like the Internet, that allows you to interact is interactive. A person who creates things is creative. Medicine that prevents disease is preventive medicine.

## Cheer for the Words

Lead the class in cheering for each word in a rhythmic way, emphasizing the morphemic parts of the word "**i-n-t-e-r—a-c-t—i-v-e**." If possible, cheer for each new word three times.

## Use the Prefixes and Suffixes

Say these sentences aloud, and have students figure out a word with one of the prefixes or suffixes—**re, inter, trans, or, ess, tion, ive**—that will make sense in the sentence.

- The person who **governs** your state is called the _____.
- In the fairy tale, the **prince** married the girl, and she became a _____.
- When people from all over the nation meet, we have a **national** meeting, but when people from all over the world meet, we have an _____ meeting.
- I can **multiply** numbers quickly, and my teacher calls me a whiz at _____.
- In order to **protect** their skin, the rescuers wore _____ clothing.
- I filed a **claim** about my stolen stereo, and when they arrested the burglars, I got to _____ it.
- When you fly over the **Atlantic** Ocean, you have made a _____ flight.

# Lesson 21

### Letters: e  i  o  c  d  r  s  v  y
### Words: dry  ride  rode  dive  diver  dries  cover  score  scored  discover  discovery

**Make Words:** Distribute the letters and tell students what words to make. After each word is made, show the correct spelling. Make sure everyone has each word spelled correctly before doing the next word. Keep the lesson fast paced.

1.  Take 3 letters and spell **dry**. I need to **dry** my hair.
2.  Use 4 letters to spell **ride**. I like to **ride** my horse.
3.  Change 1 letter to spell **rode**. Last Saturday, I **rode** all afternoon.
4.  Use 4 letters and spell **dive**. He is ready to **dive** into the pool.
5.  Add a letter to spell **diver**. He is a powerful **diver**.
6.  Use 5 letters to spell **dries**. My hair **dries** very quickly.
7.  Use 5 letters to spell **cover**. The builders put a **cover** over the hole.
8.  Use 5 letters to spell **score**. With 1 minute left, the **score** was tied.
9.  Add a letter to spell **scored**. Our star player **scored** the winning point!
10. Use 8 letters to spell **discover**. The explorers set out to **discover** new lands.
11. Now it's time for the secret word. Take a minute to see if you can figure it out. (After 1 minute, give clues if needed.) Add your letters to **discover** and spell **discovery**. Do you ever watch the **Discovery** Channel® ?

**Sort:** Display the words on cards in the order they were made, and have each word read aloud. Have the related words sorted. Talk with students about how the words are related, and have students make sentences that combine the related words.

| dry | ride | cover | dive | score |
|-----|------|-------|------|-------|
| dries | rode | discover | diver | scored |
| | | discovery | | |

**Transfer:** Have students use the related words to spell and make sentences for similar words:

**try/tries  cry/cries  agree/disagree  honest/dishonest/dishonesty**

## Word Wall Review—Be a Mind Reader (p. 141)

1.  It's one of the words on the wall.
2.  **Act** is the root word.
3.  It does not begin with the prefix trans.
4.  It means **people who act**.
5.  It means **female people who act**.

# Lesson 22

### Letters: e e o u c d n r r v
### Words: run due cover corner covered recover overrun overdue cornered uncovered undercover

**Make Words:** Distribute the letters and tell students what words to make. After each word is made, show the correct spelling. Make sure everyone has each word spelled correctly before doing the next word. Keep the lesson fast paced.

1. Take 3 letters and spell **run**. We went for a long **run**.
2. Take 3 letters and spell **due**. The payment is **due** on the first of every month.
3. Use 5 letters to spell **cover**. Please put the **cover** on the pan.
4. Use 6 letters to spell **corner.** I'll meet you at the **corner**.
5. Use 7 letters to spell **covered**. The ground was **covered** with snow.
6. Use 7 letters to spell **recover**. The robbers were caught, and we were able to **recover** most of the stolen loot.
7. Use 7 letters to spell **overrun**. The abandoned farm was **overrun** with brush and weeds.
8. Use 7 letters to spell **overdue**. She lost her job and had lots of **overdue** bills.
9. Use 8 letters to spell **cornered**. We tried to slip out without being noticed, but they **cornered** us and demanded that we tell them what we knew.
10. Use 9 letters to spell **uncovered**. Don't leave that food sitting out **uncovered**.
11. Now it's time for the secret word. Take a minute to see if you can figure it out. (After 1 minute, give clues if needed.) Add your letters to a word you have already made to spell the secret word. He was arrested by an **undercover** police officer.

**Sort:** Display the words on cards in the order they were made, and have each word read aloud. Have the related words sorted. Talk with students about how the words are related, and have students make sentences that combine the related words.

| run | due | cover | corner |
|---|---|---|---|
| overrun | overdue | covered | cornered |
| | | recover | |
| | | uncovered | |
| | | undercover | |

**Transfer:** Have students use the related words to spell and make sentences for similar words:

joy/overjoyed  shoot/overshoot  take/overtake  ground/underground

**Word Wall Review—Be a Mind Reader (p. 141)**

1. It's one of the words on the wall.
2. **Act** is the root word.
3. It has a prefix.
4. It does not begin with the prefix re.
5. It means **a business deal**.

# Lesson 23

**Letters:** a  a  e  e  e  d  p  p  r  r
**Words:** deep  read  reader  reread  appear  deeper  prepare  prepared  appeared
reappeared

**Make Words:** Distribute the letters and tell students what words to make. After each word is made, show the correct spelling. Make sure everyone has each word spelled correctly before doing the next word. Keep the lesson fast paced.

1. Take 4 letters and spell **deep**. How **deep** is the water?
2. Use 4 letters to spell **read**. What kinds of books do you **read**?
3. Use 6 letters to spell **reader**. I am a **reader** of mysteries.
4. Use the letters in reader to spell **reread**. I like to **reread** my favorite books.
5. Use 6 letters to spell **appear**. One by one, the stars **appear** in the sky.
6. Use 6 letters to spell **deeper**. The water is **deeper** on the far end of the pool.
7. Use 7 letters to spell **prepare**. I will **prepare** the snacks before the party begins.
8. Add a letter to spell **prepared**. She studied very hard and was well **prepared** for the exam.
9. Use 8 letters to spell **appeared**. My friend was late, but he finally **appeared**.
10. Now it's time for the secret word. Take a minute to see if you can figure it out. (After 1 minute, give clues if needed.) Add your letters to **appeared** to spell the secret word. The sun disappeared and then **reappeared**.

**Sort:** Display the words on cards in the order they were made, and have each word read aloud. Have the related words sorted. Talk with students about how the words are related, and have students make sentences that combine the related words.

| deep | prepare | read | appear |
|------|---------|------|--------|
| deeper | prepared | reader | appeared |
| | | reread | reappeared |

**Transfer:** Have students use the related words to spell and make sentences for similar words:

school/preschool  teen/preteen  play/replay  write/rewrite

**Word Wall Review—Be a Mind Reader (p. 141)**

1. It's one of the words on the wall.
2. Act is not the root word.
3. It has a prefix.
4. It has 11 letters.
5. It means **the opposite of magnetize**.

# Lesson 24

## Letters: a a a e e i c d n p p r s
## Words: paid ripe ripen dance dancer appear ripened prepaid disappear disappearance

**Make Words:** Distribute the letters and tell students what words to make. After each word is made, show the correct spelling. Make sure everyone has each word spelled correctly before doing the next word. Keep the lesson fast paced.

1. Take 4 letters and spell **paid**. I get **paid** every Friday.
2. Use 4 letters to spell **ripe**. The tomatoes are **ripe**.
3. Add a letter to spell **ripen**. It took forever for them to **ripen**.
4. Use 5 letters to spell **dance**. Do you like to **dance**?
5. Add a letter to spell **dancer**. You are a very good **dancer**.
6. Use 6 letters to spell **appear**. He had to **appear** in court on Monday.
7. Use 7 letters to spell **ripened**. The tomatoes **ripened** very slowly.
8. Use 7 letters to spell **prepaid**. I have **prepaid** your plane ticket.
9. Use 9 letters to spell **disappear**. The magician made the rabbit **disappear**!
10. Now it's time for the secret word. Take a minute to see if you can figure it out. (After 1 minute, give clues if needed.) Add your letters to disappear to spell the secret word. The police investigated the mysterious **disappearance** of the man.

**Sort:** Display the words on cards in the order they were made, and have each word read aloud. Have the related words sorted. Talk with students about how the words are related, and have students make sentences that combine the related words.

| | | | |
|---|---|---|---|
| appear | paid | ripe | dance |
| disappear | prepaid | ripen | dancer |
| disappearance | | ripened | |

**Transfer:** Have students use the related words to spell and make sentences for similar words:

agree/disagree like/dislike prove/disprove dark/darken/darkened

## Word Wall Review—Be a Mind Reader (p. 141)

1. It's one of the words on the wall.
2. It does not have magnet as the root word.
3. It does not have a prefix.
4. It begins with the root word **act**.
5. It is the shortest word on the wall.

# Lesson 25  Word Wall

**Word Wall Words: discovery  uncovered  undercover  reappeared  disappearance**

Give everyone a copy of the Take-Home Word Wall (p. 156) and/or place the words on the classroom Word Wall.

## Talk about the Words

Help students discover the two root words, **cover** and **appear**. Have students pronounce each word and tell what prefixes and suffixes have been added. Discuss how the prefixes and suffixes affect the meaning of the words.

**discovery:** The root word is **cover** with the prefix **dis** and the suffix **y**. **Dis** often signals an opposite meaning. When you **cover** something, you hide it. When you **discover** something, you find it. A **discovery** is something you **discover**.

**uncovered:** The root word is **cover** with the **ed** ending and the prefix **un**. **Un** also signals an opposite relationship. When you **uncover** something, you remove the **cover**.

**undercover:** The root word is **cover** with the prefix **under**. The prefix **under** often means "less" or "under." People who work **undercover** are trying not to be seen or detected.

**reappeared:** The root word is **appear** with the ending **ed** and the prefix **re**. The prefix **re** usually means "back" or "again." When something **reappears**, it **appears** again.

**disappearance:** The root word is **appear** with the prefix **dis** and the suffix **ance**. The prefix **dis** turns **appear** into the opposite—**disappear**. The suffix **ance** is often added to doing words (verbs) and changes them into naming words (nouns). When someone **disappears**, we talk about their **disappearance**.

## Cheer for the Words

Lead the class in cheering for each word in a rhythmic way, emphasizing the morphemic parts of the word "**u-n-d-e-r—c-o-v-e-r**." If possible, cheer for each new word three times.

## Use the Prefixes and Suffixes

Say these sentences aloud, and have students figure out a word with one of the prefixes or suffixes—**re**, **dis**, **un**, **under**, **y**, **ance**—that will make sense in the sentence.

- Buried deep under the **ground** was an _____ tunnel.
- They wanted to **deliver** the package and called to see if we were home so they could make the _____.
- The dancers who were going to **perform** for the president were nervous because this was their most important _____.
- The church we just **built** burned down, but we are going to _____ it.
- We didn't **expect** him to come until next month, so his visit today was very _____.
- We tried to **prove** he was innocent, but the newly discovered evidence _____ that.

## Lesson 26

**Letters:** a  e  i  o  u  c  g  g  n  n  r
**Words:** rage  race  care  canoe  raging  racing  caring  courage  uncaring  canoeing  encouraging

**Make Words:** Distribute the letters and tell students what words to make. After each word is made, show the correct spelling. Make sure everyone has each word spelled correctly before doing the next word. Keep the lesson fast paced.

1. Take 4 letters and spell **rage**. When the poisoned dog died, we felt both sorrow and **rage**.
2. Change 1 letter to spell **race**. We all went to the **race**.
3. Move the letters to spell **care**. I took **care** of my little sister.
4. Use 5 letters and spell **canoe**. Have you ever been on a **canoe** ride?
5. Use 6 letters to spell **raging**. The fire was **raging** through the woods.
6. Change 1 letter to spell **racing**. The cars were **racing** around the track.
7. Move the letters to spell **caring**. My grandma is a very **caring** person.
8. Use 7 letters to spell **courage**. The rescuers showed a lot of **courage**.
9. Use 8 letters to spell **uncaring**. The criminal was a very **uncaring** person.
10. Use 8 letters to spell **canoeing**. We went **canoeing** down the river.
11. Now it's time for the secret word. Take a minute to see if you can figure it out. (After 1 minute, give clues if needed.) Add your letters to a word you have already made and spell the secret word. Everyone was **encouraging** me to try out for the team.

**Sort:** Display the words on cards in the order they were made, and have each word read aloud. Have the related words sorted. Talk with students about how the words are related, and have students make sentences that combine the related words.

| rage | race | care | canoe | courage |
|---|---|---|---|---|
| raging | racing | caring | canoeing | encouraging |
| | | uncaring | | |

**Transfer:** Have students use the related words to spell and make sentences for similar words:

kind/unkind  dress/undress/undressing  joy/enjoy/enjoying

**Word Wall Review—Be a Mind Reader (p. 141)**

1. It's one of the words on the wall.
2. Act is not the root word.
3. **Dis** is the prefix.
4. It does not end in y.
5. It means **the opposite of appearance**.

# Lesson 27

**Letters: a e i o u c d d g r s**
**Words: radio  grace  scare  score  scored  scared  radioed  courage  gracious  disgrace discouraged**

**Make Words:** Distribute the letters and tell students what words to make. After each word is made, show the correct spelling. Make sure everyone has each word spelled correctly before doing the next word. Keep the lesson fast paced.

1. Take 5 letters and spell **radio**. <u>Do you listen to the **radio**?</u>
2. Use 5 letters and spell **grace**. <u>The dancer moved with incredible **grace**.</u>
3. Use 5 letters to spell **scare**. <u>Did the thunder **scare** the puppy?</u>
4. Change 1 letter to spell **score**. <u>The final **score** was 98-97.</u>
5. Add a letter to spell **scored**. <u>Our team **scored** the final points.</u>
6. Change 1 letter to spell **scared**. <u>The puppy was not **scared**.</u>
7. Use 7 letters to spell **radioed**. <u>The captain of the sinking ship **radioed** for help.</u>
8. Use 7 letters to spell **courage**. <u>The soldiers all showed a lot of **courage**.</u>
9. Use 8 letters to spell **gracious**. <u>The president's wife was a **gracious** hostess.</u>
10. Use 8 letters to spell **disgrace**. <u>After the scandal, the advisors left in **disgrace**.</u>
11. Now it's time for the secret word. Take a minute to see if you can figure it out. (After 1 minute, give clues if needed.) Add your letters to a word you have already made to spell the secret word. <u>Don't get **discouraged** if you can't learn to surf during the first lesson.</u>

**Sort:** Display the words on cards in the order they were made, and have each word read aloud. Have the related words sorted. Talk with students about how the words are related, and have students make sentences that combine the related words.

| radio | score | grace | scare | courage |
|---|---|---|---|---|
| radioed | scored | disgrace | scared | discouraged |
| | | gracious | | |

**Transfer:** Have students use the related words to spell and make sentences for similar words:

trust/distrust/distrusted  prove/proved/disproved  agree/disagree/disagreed

## Word Wall Review—Be a Mind Reader (p. 141)

1. It's one of the words on the wall.
2. Power is not the root word.
3. **Cover** is the root word.
4. It does not begin with the prefix dis.
5. It begins with the prefix **under**.

# Lesson 28

**Letters: a e e e o u c g m n n r t**
**Words: eat rage agree argue eaten uneaten courage outrage argument agreement encourage encouragement**

**Make Words:** Distribute the letters and tell students what words to make. After each word is made, show the correct spelling. Make sure everyone has each word spelled correctly before doing the next word. Keep the lesson fast paced.

1. Take 3 letters and spell **eat**. Let's **eat**!
2. Use 4 letters to spell **rage**. Rumpelstiltskin flew into a **rage** when his name was guessed.
3. Use 5 letters to spell **agree**. We could not **agree** on what to watch.
4. Use 5 letters to spell **argue**. I didn't want to **argue** about it.
5. Use 5 letters to spell **eaten**. When I got there, almost all of the food had been **eaten**.
6. Use 7 letters to spell **uneaten**. I quickly grabbed the **uneaten** piece of pizza.
7. Use 7 letters to spell **courage**. It took a lot of **courage** to begin riding again after the accident.
8. Use 7 letters to spell **outrage**. Everyone agreed that what they did was an **outrage**.
9. Use 8 letters to spell **argument**. My friend and I had an **argument**.
10. Use 9 letters to spell **agreement**. After much discussion, we reached an **agreement**.
11. Use 9 letters to spell **encourage**. I try to **encourage** my brother to work hard.
12. Now it's time for the secret word. Take a minute to see if you can figure it out. (After 1 minute, give clues if needed.) Add your letters to **encourage** to spell the secret word. He accepted the prize and thanked everyone for their **encouragement**.

**Sort:** Display the words on cards in the order they were made, and have each word read aloud. Have the related words sorted. Talk with students about how the words are related, and have students make sentences that combine the related words.

| eat | agree | argue | rage | courage |
|---|---|---|---|---|
| eaten | agreement | argument | outrage | encourage |
| uneaten | | | | encouragement |

**Transfer:** Have students use the related words to spell and make sentences for similar words:

enrage  enjoy/enjoyment  enrich/enrichment  enroll/enrollment

**Word Wall Review—Be a Mind Reader (p. 141)**
1. It's one of the words on the wall.
2. It has less than 9 letters.
3. It does not have the suffix or.
4. It does not end with the suffix ful.
5. It ends with the suffix **ic**.

# Lesson 29

## Letters: a e o o u u c g l r s y
### Words: cool rose rosy curl curly scare scary cooler courage courageous courageously

**Make Words:** Distribute the letters and tell students what words to make. After each word is made, show the correct spelling. Make sure everyone has each word spelled correctly before doing the next word. Keep the lesson fast paced.

1. Take 4 letters and spell **cool**. That's a **cool** bike!
2. Use 4 letters to spell **rose**. She picked a white **rose**.
3. Change 1 letter to spell **rosy**. She was in a **rosy**, cheerful mood.
4. Use 4 letters to spell **curl**. She wants to **curl** her hair.
5. Add a letter to spell **curly**. Do you like **curly** hair?
6. Use 5 letters to spell **scare**. Did the monsters in the movie **scare** you?
7. Change 1 letter to spell **scary**. I thought they were very **scary**.
8. Use 6 letters to spell **cooler**. The sodas are in the **cooler**.
9. Use 7 letters to spell **courage**. Sometimes it takes **courage** to tell the truth.
10. Add 3 letters to spell **courageous**. A person who has courage is **courageous**.
11. Now it's time for the secret word. Take a minute to see if you can figure it out. (After 1 minute, give clues if needed.) Add your letters to **courageous** to spell the secret word. All of the people behaved **courageously**.

**Sort:** Display the words on cards in the order they were made, and have each word read aloud. Have the related words sorted. Talk with students about how the words are related, and have students make sentences that combine the related words.

| cool | rose | courage | curl | scare |
|------|------|---------|------|-------|
| cooler | rosy | courageous | curly | scary |
| | | courageously | | |

**Transfer:** Have students use the related words to spell and make sentences for similar words:

rock/rocky   sudden/suddenly   honest/honesty/honestly

**Word Wall Review—Be a Mind Reader (p. 141)**

1. It's one of the words on the wall.
2. It does not have act as the root word.
3. **Cover** is the root word.
4. It has 9 letters.
5. It begins with the prefix **un**.

Give everyone a copy of the Take-Home Word Wall (p. 157) and/or place the words on the classroom Word Wall:

## Talk about the Words

Help students discover the two root words, **cover** and **appear**. Have students pronounce each word and tell what prefixes and suffixes have been added. Discuss how the prefixes and suffixes affect the meaning of the words.

**encouraging:** The root word is **courage** with the ending **ing** and the prefix **en**. The prefix **en** often means "in" or "on." When you **encourage** someone, you try to put **courage** into them. When you endanger someone, you put them in danger.

**encouragement:** The root word is **courage** with the prefix **en** and the suffix **ment**. The suffix **ment** often changes doing words (verbs) into naming words (nouns). The thing you do is "**encourage**;" the thing you give is "**encouragement**." An argument is what you have when you argue. Agreement is what you have when you agree.

**discouraged:** The root word is **courage** with the ending **ed** and the prefix **dis**. The prefix **dis** often signals an opposite—and usually a negative meaning. When you lose **courage**, you become **discouraged**. Other **dis** words on the wall include **displeased**, **discovery**, and **disappeared**.

**courageous:** The root word is **courage** with the suffix **ous**. The suffix **ous** usually means "having" or "full of." When you are **courageous**, you are full of **courage**. A dangerous place has a lot of danger. Poisonous plants have poison. Words ending in **ous** are usually describing words (adjectives).

**courageously:** The root word is **courage** with the suffixes **ous** and **ly**. The suffix **ly** often turns adjectives into adverbs. If you are **courageous**, you behave **courageously**. If you are powerful, you act powerfully.

## Cheer for the Words

Lead the class in cheering for each word in a rhythmic way, emphasizing the morphemic parts of the word "**c-o-u-r-a-g-e—o-u-s—l-y**." If possible, cheer for each new word three times.

## Use the Prefixes and Suffixes

Say these sentences aloud, and have students figure out a word with one of the prefixes or suffixes—**ous**, **ly**, **dis**, **en**, **ment**—that will make sense in the sentence.

- My brother loves **adventures** and is much more _____ than I am.
- My friend in **unemployed** and is collecting _____.
- He gave the last **correct** answer and won, because he had answered every question
_____.
- Usually my brother and I **agree** about things, but we often _____ about what to watch on TV.
- During the riots, the police had to use **force** to _____ the laws.

# Lesson 31

### Letters: a e i u g n r s t
### Words: use gain sing sign using singer signer resign regain reusing signature

**Make Words:** Distribute the letters and tell students what words to make. After each word is made, show the correct spelling. Make sure everyone has each word spelled correctly before doing the next word. Keep the lesson fast paced.

1. Take 3 letters and spell **use**. Can I **use** your eraser?
2. Use 4 letters to spell **gain**. As she got well, she began to **gain** weight.
3. Use 4 letters to spell **sing**. I like to **sing**.
4. Move the letters and spell **sign**. He didn't see the stop **sign**.
5. Use 5 letters to spell **using**. We are **using** the leftover bags and boxes.
6. Use 6 letters to spell **singer**. Who is your favorite **singer**?
7. Move the letters to spell **signer**. John Hancock was a **signer** of the Declaration of Independence.
8. Move the letters to spell **resign**. After his arrest, the chairman of the company was asked to **resign**.
9. Use 8 letters to spell **regain**. Our favorite racer fell behind, but at the very end was able to **regain** the lead.
10. Use 7 letters to spell **reusing**. We are **reusing** the decorations from last year.
11. Now it's time for the secret word. Take a minute to see if you can figure it out. (After 1 minute, give clues if needed.) Add your letters to a word you have already made and spell the secret word. The **signature** on the check did not match the **signature** on his license.

**Sort:** Display the words on cards in the order they were made, and have each word read aloud. Have the related words sorted. Talk with students about how the words are related, and have students make sentences that combine the related words.

| | | | |
|---|---|---|---|
| sign | use | gain | sing |
| signer | using | regain | singer |
| resign | reusing | | |
| signature | | | |

**Transfer:** Have students use the related words to spell and make sentences for similar words:

mix/mixture  sculpt/sculpture  place/placing/replacing

**Word Wall Review—Be a Mind Reader (p. 141)**

1. It's one of the words on the wall.
2. **Courage** is the root word.
3. En is not the prefix.
4. It has the suffix **ous**.
5. It does not have the suffix ly.

# Lesson 32

### Letters: a  e  i  i  o  g  n  n  r  s  t
### Words: rain  sign  anger  organ  resign  ignore  ignorant  organist  rainiest  angriest
### resignation

**Make Words:** Distribute the letters and tell students what words to make. After each word is made, show the correct spelling. Make sure everyone has each word spelled correctly before doing the next word. Keep the lesson fast paced.

1. Take 4 letters and spell **rain.** I hope it doesn't **rain** during our ball game.
2. Use 4 letters to spell **sign.** They communicate with **sign** language.
3. Use 5 letters to spell **anger.** I don't know how to express my **anger** at someone who would steal a wheelchair!
4. Use 5 letters to spell **organ.** She plays the **organ** at our church.
5. Use 6 letters to spell **resign.** His bad health forced him to **resign** from his job.
6. Use 6 letters to spell **ignore.** I try to **ignore** my little brother's whining, but it is not easy!
7. Use 8 letters to spell **ignorant.** Someone who doesn't know much is **ignorant.**
8. Use 8 letters to spell **organist.** The person who plays the organ is the **organist.**
9. Use 8 letters to spell **rainiest.** This was the **rainiest** summer we have ever had.
10. Use 8 letters to spell **angriest.** We were all angry, but the dog's owner was the **angriest.**
11. Now it's time for the secret word. Take a minute to see if you can figure it out. (After 1 minute, give clues if needed.) Add your letters to a word you have already made to spell the secret word. The mayor turned in his **resignation** and left town.

**Sort:** Display the words on cards in the order they were made, and have each word read aloud. Have the related words sorted. Talk with students about how the words are related, and have students make sentences that combine the related words.

| rain | organ | sign | ignore | anger |
|------|-------|------|--------|-------|
| rainiest | organist | resign | ignorant | angriest |
| | | resignation | | |

**Transfer:** Have students use the related words to spell and make sentences for similar words:

**happy/happiest  pretty/prettiest  biology/biologist  design/designation**

## Word Wall Review—Be a Mind Reader (p. 141)

1. It's one of the words on the wall.
2. **Courage** is the root word.
3. It has a prefix.
4. The prefix is **en.**
5. It ends with the suffix **ment.**

CD-2420 Big Words for Big Kids   © Carson-Dellosa

# Lesson 33

## Letters: a  e  i  g  m  n  n  s  s  t
## Words: sane  mean  meant  signs  insane  assign  magnet  magnets  meaning  assignment

**Make Words:** Distribute the letters and tell students what words to make. After each word is made, show the correct spelling. Make sure everyone has each word spelled correctly before doing the next word. Keep the lesson fast paced.

1.  Take 4 letters and spell **sane**. The psychiatrists examined her and decided she was **sane** enough to stand trial.
2.  Use 4 letters to spell **mean**. I don't think you know what I **mean**.
3.  Add a letter to spell **meant**. I **meant** to tell you I would be late.
4.  Use 5 letters to spell **signs**. We made **signs** to advertise the yard sale.
5.  Use 6 letters to spell **insane**. The opposite of sane is **insane**.
6.  Use 6 letters to spell **assign**. What did he **assign** for homework?
7.  Use 6 letters to spell **magnet**. The crumbs were a **magnet** for the ants.
8.  Add a letter to spell **magnets**. **Magnets** are things that attract other things.
9.  Use 7 letters to spell **meaning**. Sometimes I don't understand the **meaning** of words I read.
10. Now it's time for the secret word. Take a minute to see if you can figure it out. (After 1 minute, give clues if needed.) Add your letters to a word you have already made to spell the secret word. Our homework **assignment** was to interview our relatives about life when they were kids.

**Sort:** Display the words on cards in the order they were made, and have each word read aloud. Have the related words sorted. Talk with students about how the words are related, and have students make sentences that combine the related words.

| sane | signs | mean | magnet |
|---|---|---|---|
| insane | assign | meant | magnets |
|  | assignment | meaning |  |

**Transfer:** Have students use the related words to spell and make sentences for similar words:

correct/incorrect  complete/incomplete  entertain/entertainment

**Word Wall Review—Be a Mind Reader (p. 141)**

1.  It's one of the words on the wall.
2.  It has 10 letters.
3.  It is not courageous.
4.  Weight is not the root word.
5.  **Create** is the root word.

# Lesson 34

**Letters:** a  i  i  i  c  f  g  n  n  n  s  t
**Words:** act  tan  fan  scan  sign  acting  tanning  fanning  scanning  significant
insignificant

**Make Words:** Distribute the letters and tell students what words to make. After each word is made, show the correct spelling. Make sure everyone has each word spelled correctly before doing the next word. Keep the lesson fast paced.

1. Take 3 letters and spell **act**. <u>He put on a big **act**</u>!
2. Use 3 letters to spell **tan**. <u>He had a good **tan** when he came back from the beach.</u>
3. Change a letter to spell **fan**. <u>The **fan** helps us to stay cool.</u>
4. Use 4 letters to spell **scan**. <u>I am going to **scan** these pictures into my presentation.</u>
5. Use 4 letters to spell **sign**. <u>**Sign** your name here.</u>
6. Use 6 letters to spell **acting**. <u>She was **acting** very strangely.</u>
7. Use 7 letters to spell **tanning**. <u>Have you ever been to a **tanning** salon?</u>
8. Use 7 letters to spell **fanning**. <u>All of the people were **fanning** themselves and hoping the air conditioner would come back on.</u>
9. Use 8 letters to spell **scanning**. <u>I am **scanning** in the pictures.</u>
10. Use 11 letters to spell **significant**. <u>The police thought it was very **significant** that the missing person had taken her jewelry and passport.</u>
11. Now it's time for the secret word. Take a minute to see if you can figure it out. (After 1 minute, give clues if needed.) Add your letters to **significant** to spell the secret word. <u>The opposite of significant is **insignificant**.</u>

**Sort:** Display the words on cards in the order they were made, and have each word read aloud. Have the related words sorted. Talk with students about how the words are related, and have students make sentences that combine the related words.

| act | tan | sign | fan | scan |
| --- | --- | --- | --- | --- |
| acting | tanning | significant | fanning | scanning |
| | | insignificant | | |

**Transfer:** Have students use the related words to spell and make sentences for similar words:

run/running  plan/planning  act/active/inactive

## Word Wall Review—Be a Mind Reader (p. 141)

1. It's one of the words on the wall.
2. It begins with the prefix **dis**.
3. **Cover** is the root word.
4. It ends in **ed**.
5. It means **the opposite of pleased**.

Give everyone a copy of the Take-Home Word Wall (p. 158) and/or place the words on the classroom Word Wall.

## Talk about the Words

Help students discover the root word **sign**. **Sign** has a variety of meanings but all of them relate to sign, symbol, or mark. Have students pronounce each word and tell what prefixes and suffixes have been added. Discuss how the prefixes and suffixes affect the meaning of the words.

**signature:** The root word is **sign** with the suffix **ture**. When the suffix **ture** is added to **sign**, **sign** becomes a naming word (noun). We call what you **sign** your **signature**. What you mix is a mixture. Something you create is a creature.

**resignation:** The root word is **sign** with the prefix **re** and the suffix **ment**. When you **resign**, you often have to **sign** something and give back your job. **Resign** is what you do. We name what you do your **resignation**. Other similar Word Wall words are **recreation**, **reactions**, and **transaction**.

**assignment:** The root word is **sign** with the prefix **a** and the suffix **ment**. The prefix **a** often means "to" or "toward." **Assign** literally means to "sign over to." An **assignment** is the thing you are **assigned**. Encouragement is a similar **ment** word.

**significant:** The root word is **sign** with the suffix **ant**. Something that is **significant** is a **sign** of something else. If something is **significant**, it **signals** you to look more closely at it and consider various connections.

**insignificant:** The root word is **sign** with the prefix **in** and the suffix **ant**. The prefix **in** sometimes signals an opposite meaning. The opposite of **significant** is **insignificant**. The opposite of sane is insane.

## Cheer for the Words

Lead the class in cheering for each word in a rhythmic way, emphasizing the morphemic parts of the word "**i-n—s-i-g-n—i-f-i—c-a-n-t**." If possible, cheer for each new word three times.

## Use the Prefixes and Suffixes

Say these sentences aloud, and have students figure out a word with one of the prefixes or suffixes—**in**, **ant**, **ment**, **ture**, **re**, **tion**—that will make sense in the sentence.

- The **ship** pulled into the harbor with a big _____ of lumber.
- The twins had opposite reactions. Lucy was very **sensitive**, but Lulu was _____.
- She didn't like the way I had **arranged** the furniture, so she began to _____ it.
- Our team **triumphed** and had a _____ parade through town.
- The factory usually **produces** a million T-shirts a year, but this year its _____ was much lower.
- My brother is an **architect**, and his _____ is famous worldwide.

# Lesson 36

### Letters: a e i c d l m p s
### Words: deal lead medic place places placed medical mislead misdeal misplaced

**Make Words:** Distribute the letters and tell students what words to make. After each word is made, show the correct spelling. Make sure everyone has each word spelled correctly before doing the next word. Keep the lesson fast paced.

1. Take 4 letters and spell **deal**. <u>It is my turn to **deal** the cards.</u>
2. Move the letters to spell **lead**. <u>We will **lead** the parade.</u>
3. Use 5 letters to spell **medic**. <u>He was a **medic** in the army.</u>
4. Use 5 letters and spell **place**. <u>Put it back in the right **place**.</u>
5. Add a letter to spell **places**. <u>She traveled to lots of different **places**.</u>
6. Add a letter to spell **placed**. <u>She **placed** the flowers in the middle of the table.</u>
7. Use 7 letters to spell **medical**. <u>My sister is going to **medical** school to become a doctor.</u>
8. Use 7 letters to spell **mislead**. <u>The guide did not mean to **mislead** us, but we got lost anyway.</u>
9. Move the letters to spell **misdeal**. <u>If you **misdeal** the cards, they have to be dealt again.</u>
10. Now it's time for the secret word. Take a minute to see if you can figure it out. (After 1 minute, give clues if needed.) Add your letters to a word you have already made and spell the secret word. <u>The woman was very upset when she realized she had **misplaced** the important papers.</u>

**Sort:** Display the words on cards in the order they were made, and have each word read aloud. Have the related words sorted. Talk with students about how the words are related, and have students make sentences that combine the related words.

| deal | lead | medic | place |
|---|---|---|---|
| misdeal | mislead | medical | places |
| | | | placed |
| | | | misplaced |

**Transfer:** Have students use the related words to spell and make sentences for similar words:

spell/misspell  use/misuse  sign/signal

**Word Wall Review—Be a Mind Reader (p. 141)**

1. It's one of the words on the wall.
2. It has 9 letters.
3. It does not have an s ending.
4. It does not begin with the prefix un.
5. **Sign** is the root word.

# Lesson 37

## Letters: a a e e e i b c l l p r r
## Words: call race ripe riper place racial caller recall replace irreplaceable

**Make Words:** Distribute the letters and tell students what words to make. After each word is made, show the correct spelling. Make sure everyone has each word spelled correctly before doing the next word. Keep the lesson fast paced.

1. Take 4 letters and spell **call**. That phone **call** is probably for me.
2. Use 4 letters and spell **race**. Many people adopt a child from a different **race**.
3. Use 4 letters to spell **ripe**. Tomatoes are best if you wait for them to get **ripe** before you pick them.
4. Add a letter to spell **riper**. I am going to wait until these tomatoes get a little **riper**.
5. Use 5 letters to spell **place**. A **place** for everything and everything in its **place**!
6. Use 6 letters to spell **racial**. We don't have many **racial** conflicts at our school.
7. Use 6 letters to spell **caller**. Do you have **caller** ID on your phone?
8. Move the letters to spell **recall**. We were notified about a **recall** on our truck.
9. Use 7 letters to spell **replace**. I broke an old glass bowl, and I want to **replace** it.
10. Now it's time for the secret word. Take a minute to see if you can figure it out. (After 1 minute, give clues if needed.) Add your letters to **replace** to spell the secret word. The company that made the bowl was out of business, and the bowl I broke was **irreplaceable**.

**Sort:** Display the words on cards in the order they were made, and have each word read aloud. Have the related words sorted. Talk with students about how the words are related, and have students make sentences that combine the related words.

| | | | |
|---|---|---|---|
| call | race | ripe | place |
| caller | racial | riper | replace |
| recall | | | irreplaceable |

**Transfer:** Have students use the related words to spell and make sentences for similar words:

face/facial   office/official   regular/irregular

## Word Wall Review—Be a Mind Reader (p. 141)

1. It's one of the words on the wall.
2. It has the suffix **tion**.
3. It begins with the prefix **re**.
4. There is no g in the word.
5. **Act** is the root word.

# Lesson 38

### Letters: a  e  i  i  d  g  l  m  n  s
**Words: lead  deal  sign  smile  signed  signal  smiling  mislead  misdeal  signaled misdealing  misleading**

**Make Words:** Distribute the letters and tell students what words to make. After each word is made, show the correct spelling. Make sure everyone has each word spelled correctly before doing the next word. Keep the lesson fast paced.

1. Take 4 letters and spell **lead**. The **lead** dog was strong and fast.
2. Move the letters to spell **deal**. It's your turn to **deal**.
3. Use 4 letters to spell **sign**. What does that **sign** say?
4. Use 5 letters to spell **smile**. **Smile** for the camera.
5. Use 6 letters to spell **signed**. He **signed** his name to the petition.
6. Change 2 letters to spell **signal**. We sat and listened for the "all clear" **signal**.
7. Use 7 letters to spell **smiling**. She is **smiling** as if she knows something!
8. Use 7 letters to spell **mislead**. I did not mean to **mislead** you.
9. Move the letters to spell **misdeal**. When there is a **misdeal**, the next person gets to deal the cards.
10. Use 8 letters to spell **signaled**. The coach **signaled** a time-out.
11. Today there are 2 secret words. Add your letters to two words we have already made to spell the secret words. (Let students try to figure them out.) The cards were sticky so everyone was **misdealing**. It would be **misleading** to think the cards were being misdealt on purpose.

**Sort:** Display the words on cards in the order they were made, and have each word read aloud. Have the related words sorted. Talk with students about how the words are related, and have students make sentences that combine the related words.

| | | | |
|---|---|---|---|
| smile | sign | deal | lead |
| smiling | signed | misdeal | mislead |
| | signal | misdealing | misleading |
| | signaled | | |

**Transfer:** Have students use the related words to spell and make sentences for similar words:

### judge/misjudge  treat/mistreat  write/writing

**Word Wall Review—Be a Mind Reader (p. 141)**

1. It's one of the words on the wall.
2. It has 10 letters.
3. It has a suffix.
4. It has a prefix.
5. **Sign** is the root word.

CD-2420 Big Words for Big Kids

# Lesson 39

## Letters: a e e i d h l p r s
## Words: lead deal seal paid repaid sealer dealer leader leadership dealership

**Make Words:** Distribute the letters and tell students what words to make. After each word is made, show the correct spelling. Make sure everyone has each word spelled correctly before doing the next word. Keep the lesson fast paced.

1. Take 4 letters and spell **lead**. He wanted the **lead** role in the play.
2. Move the letters to spell **deal.** I got a good **deal** on a new car.
3. Change a letter to spell **seal.** You need to **seal** the cracks so water won't seep through.
4. Use 4 letters to spell **paid.** I **paid** him the money I owed him.
5. Add 2 letters to spell **repaid.** I **repaid** all of the money I borrowed.
6. Use 6 letters to spell **sealer.** You can use a **sealer** to seal the cracks.
7. Change a letter to spell **dealer.** The car **dealer** was making everyone good deals.
8. Move the letters to spell **leader.** Follow the **leader**.
9. There are 2 secret words again today. Add your letters to two words we have already made to spell the secret words. (Let students try to figure them out.) All of the dealers were trying to sell the most cars, but because of my dad's **leadership** his **dealership** was leading.

**Sort:** Display the words on cards in the order they were made, and have each word read aloud. Have the related words sorted. Talk with students about how the words are related, and have students make sentences that combine the related words.

| | | | |
|---|---|---|---|
| seal | deal | paid | lead |
| sealer | dealer | repaid | leader |
| | dealership | | leadership |

**Transfer:** Have students use the related words to spell and make sentences for similar words:

friend/friendship  member/membership  sports/sportsmanship

## Word Wall Review—Be a Mind Reader (p. 141)

1. It's one of the words on the wall.
2. **Sign** is the root word.
3. It begins with a prefix.
4. It has 11 letters.
5. It means **the opposite of significant**.

# Lesson 40  Word Wall

**Word Wall Words: irreplaceable  misplaced  misleading  leadership  dealership**

Give everyone a copy of the Take-Home Word Wall (p. 159) and/or place the words on the classroom Word Wall.

## Talk about the Words

Help students discover the root words, **place, lead**, and **deal**. Have students pronounce each word and tell what prefixes and suffixes have been added. Discuss how the prefixes and suffixes affect the meaning of the words.

**irreplaceable:** The root word is **place** with the prefixes **ir** and **re** and the suffix **able**. When you replace something, you can place it back or have it again. The prefix **ir** is used before words beginning with r to turn them into an opposite—irregular, irrational. Something you are unable to **replace** is **irreplaceable**.

**misplaced:** The root word is **place** with the prefix **mis** and the ending **ed**. The prefix **mis** often indicates a "wrong" or a "mistake." When you **misplace** something, you place it in the wrong **place** and then can't find it. When you misdeal, you make a mistake and give someone too many or too few cards.

**misleading:** The root word is **lead** with the prefix **mis** and the ending **ing**. When you **mislead** someone, you **lead** them in the wrong direction—sometimes intentionally.

**leadership:** The root word is **lead** with the suffixes **er** and **ship**. The suffix **er** often indicates a person or thing that does something. The **leader leads**. The suffix **ship** indicates a shared quality related to the root word. **Leadership** is the quality **leaders** share. Friendship is what friends share.

**dealership:** The root word is **deal** with the suffixes **er** and **ship**. A person who makes **deals** is a **dealer**. The business that all of the **dealers** share is called the **dealership**.

## Cheer for the Words

Lead the class in cheering for each word in a rhythmic way emphasizing the morphemic parts of the word "**d-e-a-l—e-r—s-h-i-p**." If possible, cheer for each new word three times.

## Use the Prefixes and Suffixes

Say these sentences aloud, and have students figure out a word with one of the prefixes or suffixes—**mis**, **ship**, **ir**—that will make sense in the sentence.

- Our team became the **champions** when they won the state _____.
- My dad and his brother have been business **partners** for many years and have a very successful _____.
- She has always been a **responsible** person, but her behavior at the party was very
  _____.
- I tried to **understand** what he wanted done, but he was not happy with my work, and I realized we had a huge _____.
- I thought the information was very **relevant**, but the judge wouldn't allow me to testify about it because she said it was _____.

CD-2420 Big Words for Big Kids © Carson-Dellosa

# Lesson 41

### Letters: e e e i d d n n p t
**Words:** diet edit edited dieted indent intend depend indented intended dependent independent

**Make Words:** Distribute the letters and tell students what words to make. After each word is made, show the correct spelling. Make sure everyone has each word spelled correctly before doing the next word. Keep the lesson fast paced.

1. Take 4 letters and spell **diet**. We are all on a **diet**.
2. Move the letters to spell **edit**. Will you help me **edit** my story?
3. Add 2 letters to spell **edited**. They **edited** the story together.
4. Move the letters and spell **dieted**. She **dieted** for three months before the wedding.
5. Use 6 letters to spell **indent**. You need to **indent** this paragraph.
6. Move the letters to spell **intend**. When do you **intend** to finish that?
7. Use 6 letters to spell **depend**. I **depend** on my friends to help me.
8. Use 8 letters to spell **indented**. Check to see if you have **indented** all of the paragraphs.
9. Move the letters to spell **intended**. She **intended** to come, but she got sick.
10. Use 9 letters to spell **dependent**. My grandma doesn't like being **dependent** on other people.
11. Now it's time for the secret word. Take a minute to see if you can figure it out. (After 1 minute, give clues if needed.) Add your letters to **dependent** and spell the secret word. My grandma is a very **independent** woman.

**Sort:** Display the words on cards in the order they were made, and have each word read aloud. Have the related words sorted. Talk with students about how the words are related, and have students make sentences that combine the related words.

| edit | diet | depend | intend | indent |
|------|------|--------|--------|--------|
| edited | dieted | dependent | intended | indented |
| | | independent | | |

**Transfer:** Have students use the related words to spell and make sentences for similar words:

depend/depended  assign/assigned  formal/informal

**Word Wall Review—Be a Mind Reader (p. 141)**

1. It is in the first half of the alphabet (**A-M**).
2. It has 10 letters.
3. Bright is not the root word.
4. **Lead** is the root word.
5. It begins with the prefix **mis**.

# Lesson 42

### Letters: e e e i c d d n n p
### Words: end need deep ended needed depend deepen deepened dependence independence

**Make Words:** Distribute the letters and tell students what words to make. After each word is made, show the correct spelling. Make sure everyone has each word spelled correctly before doing the next word. Keep the lesson fast paced.

1. Take 3 letters and spell **end**. <u>I am almost to the **end** of the book.</u>
2. Use 4 letters and spell **need**. <u>Do you **need** anything?</u>
3. Use 4 letters to spell **deep**. <u>How **deep** is the water?</u>
4. Use 5 letters to spell **ended**. <u>The book **ended** happily.</u>
5. Use 6 letters to spell **needed**. <u>I **needed** money for lunch.</u>
6. Use 6 letters to spell **depend**. <u>The grade I get will **depend** on how I do on this test.</u>
7. Use 6 letters to spell **deepen**. <u>They measured the hole and decided they had to **deepen** it.</u>
8. Add 2 letters to spell **deepened**. <u>They **deepened** it two more feet.</u>
9. Use 10 letters to spell **dependence**. <u>Many people see the **dependence** of the United States on other countries for its oil as a growing threat.</u>
10. Now it's time for the secret word. Take a minute to see if you can figure it out. (After 1 minute, give clues if needed.) Add your letters to **dependence** to spell the secret word. <u>Thomas Jefferson wrote the Declaration of **Independence**.</u>

**Sort:** Display the words on cards in the order they were made, and have each word read aloud. Have the related words sorted. Talk with students about how the words are related, and have students make sentences that combine the related words.

| end | need | deep | depend |
|-----|------|------|--------|
| ended | needed | deepen | dependence |
| | | deepened | independence |

**Transfer:** Have students use the related words to spell and make sentences for similar words:

**fright/frighten/frightened exist/existence differ/difference**

**Word Wall Review—Be a Mind Reader (p. 141)**

1. It is in the first half of the alphabet (**A-M**).
2. It has 10 letters.
3. It does not have a prefix.
4. It ends in the suffix **ship**.
5. **Lead** is the root word.

# Lesson 43

### Letters: a  a  e  i  i  o  l  n  n  n  r  t  t
### Words: rot  rent  alter  rental  rotten  nation  national  tolerant  intolerant  alteration
### international

**Make Words:** Distribute the letters and tell students what words to make. After each word is made, show the correct spelling. Make sure everyone has each word spelled correctly before doing the next word. Keep the lesson fast paced.

1. Take 3 letters and spell **rot**. If you leave that out in the sun too long, it will **rot**.
2. Use 4 letters to spell **rent**. We **rent** an apartment.
3. Use 5 letters to spell **alter**. When someone got sick, everyone else had to **alter** their schedules to cover for the sick person.
4. Use 6 letters to spell **rental**. Avis® and Hertz® are **rental** car agencies.
5. Use 6 letters to spell **rotten**. This apple is **rotten**.
6. Use 6 letters to spell **nation**. This **nation** is the United States of America.
7. Add 2 letters to spell **national**. My brother is in the **national** guard.
8. Use 8 letters to spell **tolerant**. We all try to be **tolerant** of the rights of others.
9. Add 2 letters to spell **intolerant**. The opposite of tolerant is **intolerant**.
10. Use 10 letters to spell **alteration**. When you alter something, you make an **alteration**.
11. Now it's time for the secret word. Take a minute to see if you can figure it out. (After 1 minute, give clues if needed.) Add your letters to a word we have already made to spell the secret word. Global warming is an **international** problem.

**Sort:** Display the words on cards in the order they were made, and have each word read aloud. Have the related words sorted. Talk with students about how the words are related, and have students make sentences that combine the related words.

| rent | alter | rot | tolerant | nation |
|------|-------|-----|----------|--------|
| rental | alteration | rotten | intolerant | national |
| | | | | international |

**Transfer:** Have students use the related words to spell and make sentences for similar words:

### mission/intermission  person/personal  hid/hidden

## Word Wall Review—Be a Mind Reader (p. 141)

1. It is in the last half of the alphabet (**N-Z**).
2. It has a prefix.
3. It begins with the letter **r**.
4. It has the suffix **tion**.
5. **Create** is the root word.

# Lesson 44

### Letters: a a e i i i o l n n s t t
### Words: list alien steal stole stolen enlist nation national alienation nationalities

**Make Words:** Distribute the letters and tell students what words to make. After each word is made, show the correct spelling. Make sure everyone has each word spelled correctly before doing the next word. Keep the lesson fast paced.

1. Take 4 letters and spell **list**. Put my name on the **list**.
2. Use 5 letters to spell **alien.** An **alien** is a person who comes from one country, but lives in a different country.
3. Use 5 letters to spell **steal**. It is wrong to **steal**.
4. Use 5 letters to spell **stole**. Someone **stole** my bike.
5. Add 1 letter to spell **stolen**. They found my **stolen** bike behind an old shed.
6. Use 6 letters to spell **enlist**. When he is 18, he can **enlist** in the navy.
7. Use 6 letters to spell **nation**. What **nation** do they come from?
8. Add 2 letters to spell **national**. Our **national** teams compete in the Olympics.
9. Use 10 letters to spell **alienation**. When my grandparents first came to the United States, they suffered feelings of homesickness and **alienation**.
10. Now it's time for the secret word. Take a minute to see if you can figure it out. (After 1 minute, give clues if needed.) Add your letters to a word we have already made to spell the secret word. People from many different **nationalities** live and work together in this country.

**Sort:** Display the words on cards in the order they were made, and have each word read aloud. Have the related words sorted. Talk with students about how the words are related, and have students make sentences that combine the related words.

| list | alien | steal | nation |
| enlist | alienation | stole | national |
| | | stolen | nationalities |

**Transfer:** Have students use the related words to spell and make sentences for similar words:

act/enact rage/enrage person/personal/personalities

**Word Wall Review—Be a Mind Reader (p. 141)**

1. It is in the first half of the alphabet (**A-M**).
2. It does not have a prefix.
3. It begins with the letter **c**.
4. **Courage** is the root word.
5. It has two suffixes.

# Lesson 45 Word Wall

**Word Wall Words: independent  independence  national  international  nationalities**

Give everyone a copy of the Take-Home Word Wall (p. 160) and/or place the words on the classroom Word Wall:

## Talk about the Words

Help students discover the root words, **depend** and **nation**. Have students pronounce each word and tell what prefixes and suffixes have been added. Discuss how the prefixes and suffixes affect the meaning of the words.

**independent:** The root word is **depend** with the prefix **in** and the suffix **ent**. When you **depend** on someone or something, you are **dependent**. **In** changes **dependent** into the opposite, **independent**.

**independence:** The root word is **depend** with the prefix **in** and the suffix **ence**. When you **depend** on someone or something, you are in a state of **dependence**. **In** changes **dependence** into the opposite, **independence**.

**national:** The root word is **nation** with the suffix **al**. The suffix **al** often changes naming words (nouns) to describing words (adjectives). When we talk about a problem a **nation** has, we are talking about a **national** problem.

**international:** The root word is **nation** with the prefix **inter** and the suffix **al**. The prefix **inter** means "between." **International** problems are shared between many nations.

**nationalities:** The root word is **nation** with the suffix **al**, the suffix **ity** and the ending **es** (y changes to i). **Nationality** refers to the country people originated from. Irish, Italian, French, Chinese, and Mexican are just a few of the many **nationalities** that make up the population of this **nation**.

## Cheer for the Words

Lead the class in cheering for each word in a rhythmic way, emphasizing the morphemic parts of the word "**n-a-t-i-o-n—a-l—i-t-i-e-s**." If possible, cheer for each new word three times.

## Use the Prefixes and Suffixes

Say these sentences aloud, and have students figure out a word with one of the prefixes or suffixes—**in**, **ent**, **ence**, **al**, **inter**—that will make sense in the sentence.

- Because people **differ** on so many things, we say that everyone is _____.
- I **prefer** butter pecan ice cream, but it is your birthday, so we will buy your

  _____.
- A highway that goes between different **states** is an _____ highway.
- The electricity does not go off very **frequently**. In fact, I would say it happens quite

  _____.
- She grew up in the **tropics** and now spends every vacation in _____ countries.

# Lesson 46

### Letters: a e e i h h l r t
### Words: tie heal heat late later retie reheat heater healer health healthier

**Make Words:** Distribute the letters and tell students what words to make. After each word is made, show the correct spelling. Make sure everyone has each word spelled correctly before doing the next word. Keep the lesson fast paced.

1. Take 3 letters and spell **tie**. <u>**Tie** your shoes.</u>
2. Use 4 letters to spell **heal**. <u>I broke my arm, but it is starting to **heal**.</u>
3. Change 1 letter to spell **heat**. <u>Turn on the **heat**.</u>
4. Use 4 letters and spell **late**. <u>She was **late** for school.</u>
5. Add a letter to spell **later**. <u>Our bus broke down, and we got to school even **later**.</u>
6. Use 5 letters to spell **retie**. <u>**Retie** your shoes.</u>
7. Use 6 letters to spell **reheat**. <u>My coffee got cold, so I am going to **reheat** it.</u>
8. Move the letters to spell **heater**. <u>The **heater** is not working.</u>
9. Change 1 letter to spell **healer**. <u>The medicine man was a **healer**.</u>
10. Change 2 letters to spell **health**. <u>Exercise and eating right are important for good **health**.</u>
11. Now it's time for the secret word. Take a minute to see if you can figure it out. (After 1 minute, give clues if needed.) Add your letters to **health** and spell the secret word. <u>I am eating better now and I feel **healthier**.</u>

**Sort:** Display the words on cards in the order they were made, and have each word read aloud. Have the related words sorted. Talk with students about how the words are related, and have students make sentences that combine the related words.

| | | | |
|---|---|---|---|
| tie | heat | late | heal |
| retie | reheat | later | healer |
| | heater | | health |
| | | | healthier |

**Transfer:** Have students use the related words to spell and make sentences for similar words:

pretty/prettier happy/happier paint/repaint write/rewrite

## Word Wall Review—Be a Mind Reader (p. 141)

1. It is in the first half of the alphabet (**A-M**).
2. It has 11 or more letters.
3. It has a prefix and a suffix.
4. **Depend** is the root word.
5. It is **the opposite of dependent**.

# Lesson 47

### Letters: a e e i u h h l n s t t
### Words: tie neat heal untie health neatest hesitate hesitant healthiest unhealthiest

**Make Words:** Distribute the letters and tell students what words to make. After each word is made, show the correct spelling. Make sure everyone has each word spelled correctly before doing the next word. Keep the lesson fast paced.

1. Take 3 letters and spell **tie**. I do not know how to **tie** a slip knot.
2. Use 4 letters and spell **neat**. My mom likes everything to be clean and **neat**.
3. Use 4 letters to spell **heal**. Is that cut starting to **heal**?
4. Use 5 letters to spell **untie**. Can you **untie** this knot?
5. Use 6 letters to spell **health**. She is not in very good **health**.
6. Use 7 letters to spell **neatest**. I wonder who has the **neatest** desk?
7. Use 8 letters to spell **hesitate**. He did not **hesitate** to give his opinion.
8. Change 2 letters to spell **hesitant**. The shy boy was **hesitant** to talk.
9. Use 9 letters to spell **healthiest**. I am going to buy this plant because it looks the **healthiest**.
10. Now it's time for the secret word. Take a minute to see if you can figure it out. (After 1 minute, give clues if needed.) Add your letters to **healthiest** to spell the secret word. The opposite of healthiest is **unhealthiest**.

**Sort:** Display the words on cards in the order they were made, and have each word read aloud. Have the related words sorted. Talk with students about how the words are related, and have students make sentences that combine the related words.

| tie | hesitate | neat | heal |
|-----|----------|------|------|
| untie | hesitant | neatest | health |
| | | | healthiest |
| | | | unhealthiest |

**Transfer:** Have students use the related words to spell and make sentences for similar words:

tolerate/tolerant vacate/vacant happy/happiest/unhappiest

**Word Wall Review—Be a Mind Reader (p. 141)**

1. It is in the first half of the alphabet (**A-M**).
2. It has 10 letters.
3. It has a prefix.
4. It has a suffix.
5. **Sign** is the root word.

# Lesson 48

**Letters: a a i i i o c c f l n s s t**
**Words: class final social classic fiction fictional finalists socialist antisocial classification**

**Make Words:** Distribute the letters and tell students what words to make. After each word is made, show the correct spelling. Make sure everyone has each word spelled correctly before doing the next word. Keep the lesson fast paced.

1. Take 5 letters and spell **class**. <u>The **class** of 1994 was having a reunion.</u>
2. Use 5 letters to spell **final**. <u>We are playing in the **final** game of the season.</u>
3. Use 6 letters to spell **social**. <u>She was a very **social** person who had lots of friends.</u>
4. Use 7 letters to spell **classic**. <u>My uncle collects **classic** cars.</u>
5. Use 7 letters to spell **fiction**. <u>I like to read historical **fiction**.</u>
6. Add 2 letters to spell **fictional**. <u>The characters were all **fictional**, but they seemed very real.</u>
7. Use 9 letters to spell **finalists**. <u>There were four **finalists** in the last round of the math competition.</u>
8. Use 9 letters to spell **socialist**. <u>Many countries in Europe have **socialist** governments.</u>
9. Use 10 letters to spell **antisocial**. <u>Someone who doesn't like people is **antisocial**.</u>
10. Now it's time for the secret word. Take a minute to see if you can figure it out. (Wait 1 minute and then give clues.) Add your letters to a word we have already made to spell the secret word. <u>In science, we learn about the **classification** of plants and animals.</u>

**Sort:** Display the words on cards in the order they were made, and have each word read aloud. Have the related words sorted. Talk with students about how the words are related, and have students make sentences that combine the related words.

| | | | |
|---|---|---|---|
| fiction | final | social | class |
| fictional | finalists | socialist | classic |
| | | antisocial | classification |

**Transfer:** Have students use the related words to spell and make sentences for similar words:

freeze/antifreeze   biology/biologist   tour/tourist   modify/modification

**Word Wall Review—Be a Mind Reader (p. 141)**

1. It is in the last half of the alphabet (**N-Z**).
2. It does not have a prefix.
3. Sign is not the root word.
4. **Nation** is the root word.
5. It has 13 letters.

# Lesson 49

## Letters: a e i c d f l s s y
## Words: lady safe side aside class classy safely ladies classify declassify

**Make Words:** Distribute the letters and tell students what words to make. After each word is made, show the correct spelling. Make sure everyone has each word spelled correctly before doing the next word. Keep the lesson fast paced.

1. Take 4 letters and spell **lady**. We call the wife of a president the first **lady**.
2. Use 4 letters to spell **safe**. We thought the runner was out, but the umpire ruled that he was **safe**.
3. Use 4 letters to spell **side**. We walked along the **side** of the road.
4. Add a letter to spell **aside**. When we came in, she put her work **aside** and made us welcome.
5. Use 5 letters to spell **class**. Which **class** are you in?
6. Add a letter to spell **classy**. She is a very **classy** dresser.
7. Use 6 letters to spell **safely**. I am teaching my brother how to cross streets **safely**.
8. Use 6 letters to spell **ladies**. We helped the **ladies** out of the vans.
9. Use 8 letters to spell **classify**. No one knew what had really happened because the government decided to **classify** the letters.
10. Now it's time for the secret word. Take a minute to see if you can figure it out. (After 1 minute, give clues if needed.) Add your letters to **classify** to spell the secret word. When they **declassify** the letters, we will be able to figure out what happened.

**Sort:** Display the words on cards in the order they were made, and have each word read aloud. Have the related words sorted. Talk with students about how the words are related, and have students make sentences that combine the related words.

| lady | safe | side | class |
|------|------|------|-------|
| ladies | safely | aside | classy |
| | | | classify |
| | | | declassify |

**Transfer:** Have students use the related words to spell and make sentences for similar words:

puppy/puppies   bunny/bunnies   round/around   cross/across

**Word Wall Review—Be a Mind Reader (p. 141)**

1. It is in the first half of the alphabet (**A-M**).
2. It has a prefix and a suffix.
3. It begins with the letter **i**.
4. **Inter** is the prefix.
5. It means **between nations**.

# Lesson 50 Word Wall

## Word Wall Words: healthier unhealthiest classic declassify classification

Give everyone a copy of the Take-Home Word Wall (p. 161) and/or place the words on the classroom Word Wall:

## Talk about the Words

Help students discover the root words, **health** and **class**. Have students pronounce each word and tell what prefixes and suffixes have been added. Discuss how the prefixes and suffixes affect the meaning of the words.

**healthier:** The root word is **health** with the suffixes **y—changed to i** with **er** added. **Healthy** is a word used to describe people who have good **health**. **Healthier** means more **healthy**.

**unhealthiest:** The root word is **health** with the prefix **un** and the suffixes **y—changed to i** with **est** added. **Unhealthy** is the opposite of **healthy**. The **unhealthiest** people are the most **unhealthy** people.

**classic:** The root word is **class** with the suffix **ic**. The word **classic** is often used to describe something that is the best in its **class**.

**declassify:** The root word is **class** with the prefix **de** and the suffix **ify**. The suffix **ify** means "to make something a certain way." When you make something a certain **class**, you **classify** it. **Declassify** takes away the **classified** status in the same way that demagnetize takes away the magnetism.

**classification:** The root word is **class** with the suffixes **ify (y changes to i)** and **tion**. **Classify** is what you do (verb). **Classification** is what you have (noun) when you have **classified**.

## Cheer for the Words

Lead the class in cheering for each word in a rhythmic way, emphasizing the morphemic parts of the word "**c-l-a-s-s—i-f-i—c-a-t-i-o-n**." If possible, cheer for each new word three times.

## Use the Prefixes and Suffixes

Say these sentences aloud, and have students figure out a word with one of the prefixes or suffixes—**un**, **er**, **est**, **de**, **ify**, **tion**—that will make sense in the sentence.

- My dad is an **inventor**, and he has created some amazing _____.
- My boss believes in keeping things **simple**, so I am looking for ways to _____ all of our operations.
- I have seen some **strange** movies, but this is the _____ movie ever!
- We had a **cold** winter last year, but this winter is even _____.
- We **activated** the emergency drought plan, but after three days of rain, we _____ it.
- He was very **successful**, but unfortunately, his sister was very _____.

# Lesson 51

### Letters: e e i d g n p r s s
**Words: sign press signed design pressed depress designer redesign pressing depressing**

**Make Words:** Distribute the letters and tell students what words to make. After each word is made, show the correct spelling. Make sure everyone has each word spelled correctly before doing the next word. Keep the lesson fast paced.

1. Take 4 letters and spell **sign**. Let's make a **sign** for the rally.
2. Use 5 letters to spell **press**. **Press** that button, and the door will open.
3. Use 6 letters to spell **signed**. We **signed** all of the papers and drove our new car home.
4. Move the letters and spell **design**. I like to **design** clothes.
5. Use 7 letters to spell **pressed**. We **pressed** the button, but nothing happened.
6. Move the letters to spell **depress**. I try not to let things **depress** me.
7. Use 8 letters to spell **designer**. When I grow up, I am going to be a fashion **designer**.
8. Move the letters to spell **redesign**. If I design something and then I don't like it, I just **redesign** it.
9. Use 8 letters to spell **pressing**. When I have a headache, it feels like something is **pressing** on my head.
10. Now it's time for the secret word. Take a minute to see if you can figure it out. (After 1 minute, give clues if needed.) Add your letters to **pressing** and spell the secret word. Six rainy days in a row can be very **depressing**!

**Sort:** Display the words on cards in the order they were made, and have each word read aloud. Have the related words sorted. Talk with students about how the words are related, and have students make sentences that combine the related words.

| | |
|---|---|
| sign | press |
| signed | pressed |
| design | depress |
| designer | pressing |
| redesign | depressing |

**Transfer:** Have students use the related words to spell and make sentences for similar words:

form/formed/deformed  compose/composed/decomposed

## Word Wall Review—Be a Mind Reader (p. 141)

1. It is in the last half of the alphabet (**N-Z**).
2. It has a prefix.
3. It begins with the letter **u**.
4. **Un** is the prefix.
5. It is **the opposite of healthiest**.

# Lesson 52

### Letters: e e i o n p r s s x
### Words: open pose ripe ripen press opener reopen expose express expression

**Make Words:** Distribute the letters and tell students what words to make. After each word is made, show the correct spelling. Make sure everyone has each word spelled correctly before doing the next word. Keep the lesson fast paced.

1. Take 4 letters and spell **open**. What time does the store **open**?
2. Use 4 letters and spell **pose**. I don't like to **pose** for pictures.
3. Use 4 letters to spell **ripe**. The strawberries are not **ripe**.
4. Add a letter to spell **ripen.** When do you think they will **ripen**?
5. Use 5 letters to spell **press**. You have to **press** down and turn to open that.
6. Use 6 letters to spell **opener**. Where is the can **opener**?
7. Move the letters to spell **reopen**. The store that had the fire is going to **reopen**.
8. Use 6 letters to spell **expose**. The reporter wrote the article to **expose** the truth.
9. Use 7 letters to spell **express**. When the little girl was located, the parents found it hard to **express** how grateful they were to all of the volunteers.
10. Now it's time for the secret word. Take a minute to see if you can figure it out. (After 1 minute, give clues if needed.) Add your letters to **express** to spell the secret word. They donated money to the community center as an **expression** of their gratitude.

**Sort:** Display the words on cards in the order they were made, and have each word read aloud. Have the related words sorted. Talk with students about how the words are related, and have students make sentences that combine the related words.

| | | | |
|---|---|---|---|
| ripe | open | pose | press |
| ripen | opener | expose | express |
| | reopen | | expression |

**Transfer:** Have students use the related words to spell and make sentences for similar words:

port/export/exporter   impress/impression   repress/repression

**Word Wall Review—Be a Mind Reader (p. 141)**

1. It is in the first half of the alphabet (**A-M**).
2. It does not have a prefix.
3. It begins with a **c**.
4. It has 7 letters.
5. **Class** is the root word.

# Lesson 53

### Letters: e e i i u m n p r s s v
**Words:** pure  sure  press  virus  impure  insure  ensure  viruses  impress  impressive unimpressive

**Make Words:** Distribute the letters and tell students what words to make. After each word is made, show the correct spelling. Make sure everyone has each word spelled correctly before doing the next word. Keep the lesson fast paced.

1. Take 4 letters and spell **pure**. When making prescription drugs, the ingredients have to be very **pure**.
2. Change 1 letter to spell **sure**. I want to be **sure** this package gets to my aunt.
3. Use 5 letters to spell **press**. **Press** the sides down and put tape all around.
4. Use 5 letters to spell **virus**. She was sick with a **virus**.
5. Use 6 letters to spell **impure**. The opposite of pure is **impure**.
6. Use 6 letters to spell **insure**. I am going to **insure** this package before I mail it.
7. Change 1 letter to spell **ensure**. Insuring it will not **ensure** that it gets there, but if it doesn't arrive, the insurance money will let me replace it.
8. Use 7 letters to spell **viruses**. People and computers can get **viruses**.
9. Use 7 letters to spell **impress**. The girl wanted to **impress** the boy with her baking ability, so she baked brownies for him.
10. Add 3 letters to spell **impressive**. Her ability to bake was quite **impressive**.
11. Now it's time for the secret word. Take a minute to see if you can figure it out. (After 1 minute, give clues if needed.) Add your letters to **impressive** to spell the secret word. The opposite of impressive is **unimpressive**.

**Sort:** Display the words on cards in the order they were made, and have each word read aloud. Have the related words sorted. Talk with students about how the words are related, and have students make sentences that combine the related words.

| pure | sure | virus | press |
|------|------|-------|-------|
| impure | insure | viruses | impress |
| | ensure | | impressive |
| | | | unimpressive |

**Transfer:** Have students use the related words to spell and make sentences for similar words:

perfect/imperfect  possible/impossible  mature/immature

## Word Wall Review—Be a Mind Reader (p. 141)

1. It is in the last half of the alphabet (**N-Z**).
2. It does not have a prefix.
3. Power is not the root word.
4. **Nation** is the root word.
5. It has 8 letters.

# Lesson 54

**Letters:** e e i u d p r r s s z

**Words:** press seize seized seizure pressed depress repress pressure pressured pressurized

**Make Words:** Distribute the letters and tell students what words to make. After each word is made, show the correct spelling. Make sure everyone has each word spelled correctly before doing the next word. Keep the lesson fast paced.

1. Take 5 letters and spell **press**. The newspaper was printed on the printing **press**.
2. Use 5 letters to spell **seize**. The police could **seize** the property of the criminals.
3. Add a letter to spell **seized**. They **seized** a truck and a boat.
4. Use 7 letters to spell **seizure**. The girl had an epileptic **seizure**.
5. Use 7 letters to spell **pressed**. We **pressed** the button and the door opened.
6. Move the letters to spell **depress**. I knew the bad news would **depress** him.
7. Change a letter to spell **repress**. When something truly terrifying happens, you sometimes **repress** the memory of it.
8. Use 8 letters to spell **pressure**. As we climbed higher and higher, it became harder and harder to breathe because of the low air **pressure**.
9. Add a letter to spell **pressured**. I wanted to leave, but my friends **pressured** me to stay.
10. Now it's time for the secret word. Take a minute to see if you can figure it out. (After 1 minute, give clues if needed.) Add your letters to a word you have already made to spell the secret word. The air in the airplane cabin was **pressurized** so we could fly at very high altitudes.

**Sort:** Display the words on cards in the order they were made, and have each word read aloud. Have the related words sorted. Talk with students about how the words are related, and have students make sentences that combine the related words.

| | |
|---|---|
| seize | press |
| seized | pressed |
| seizure | depress |
| | repress |
| | pressure |
| | pressured |
| | pressurized |

**Transfer:** Have students use the related words to spell and make sentences for similar words:

**expose/exposure   fail/failure   please/pleasure**

**Word Wall Review—Be a Mind Reader (p. 141)**

1. It is in the first half of the alphabet (**A-M**).
2. It has a prefix and a suffix.
3. It begins with the letter **d**.
4. **De** is the prefix.
5. **Class** is the root word.

# Lesson 55  Word Wall

**Word Wall Words: depressing  expression  repress  unimpressive  pressurized**

Give everyone a copy of the Take-Home Word Wall (p. 162) and/or place the words on the classroom Word Wall.

## Talk about the Words

Help students discover the root word **press**. Have students pronounce each word and tell what prefixes and suffixes have been added. Discuss how the prefixes and suffixes affect the meanings of the words.

**depressing:** The root word is **press** with the prefix **de** and the **ing** ending. The prefix **de** sometimes means "down." Something that is **depressing presses** you down. When you descend, you go down. When you degrade something, you grade it down.

**expression:** The root word is **press** with the prefix **ex** and the suffix **sion**. The prefix **ex** sometimes means "out." When you **express** something, you **press** it out. The **expression** in your voice and face often shows to the outside world how you feel. When you exit, you go out.

**repress:** The root word is **press** with the prefix **re**, meaning "back." Sometimes people are hypnotized to bring back **repressed** memories—memories they have pressed back and can't easily recall. **Repressive** governments press back the words and thoughts of people.

**unimpressive:** The root word is **press** with the prefixes **un** and **in** and the suffix **ive**. When you try to **impress** someone, you try to **press** into them how great you are! Something that is **impressive** makes a good **impression** on everyone who sees it. **Unimpressive** is the opposite of **impressive**.

**pressurized:** The root word is **press** with the suffixes **sure** and **ize** and the **ed** ending. Things that are **pressed** together have **pressure**. When you **pressurize** something, you make it have **pressure**, just as when you magnetize something, you make it magnetic.

## Cheer for the Words

Lead the class in cheering for each word in a rhythmic way emphasizing the morphemic parts of the word "**p-r-e-s-s—u-r—i-z-e-d.**" If possible, cheer for each new word three times.

## Use the Prefixes and Suffixes

Say these sentences aloud, and have students figure out a word with one of the prefixes or suffixes—**de**, **ex**, **re**, **im**, **un**, **ize**—that will make sense in the sentence.

* My mom helped me make a list of all the guests we should **include** because I didn't want to _____ anyone and hurt their feelings.
* The lieutenant was **promoted** because of his bravery, but he was later _____ for lying to his superiors.
* The money my dad loaned me helped me **pay** my bills, but now I am saving so that I can _____him.
* The businessman traveled all over the world arranging to **export** and _____ products.
* I am usually a **lucky** person, but this week I have been very _____.
* My mother is a hard-nosed **critic,** but I know she just means to help and doesn't mean to _____ me.

## Lesson 56

### Letters: a e e o c f m n p r r
### Words: farm form camp force camper farmer reform enforce perform performance

**Make Words:** Distribute the letters and tell students what words to make. After each word is made, show the correct spelling. Make sure everyone has each word spelled correctly before doing the next word. Keep the lesson fast paced.

1. Take 4 letters and spell **farm**. We went to the **farm** to pick corn.
2. Change 1 letter to spell **form**. The line began to **form** at daybreak.
3. Use 4 letters to spell **camp**. In the summer, we go to **camp**.
4. Use 5 letters and spell **force**. The police had to use **force** to disperse the crowd.
5. Use 6 letters to spell **camper**. Everyone spread out to look for the lost **camper**.
6. Use 6 letters to spell **farmer**. The **farmer** plowed the fields with his tractor.
7. Use 6 letters to spell **reform**. After the scandal, the mayor promised he would **reform** the police department.
8. Use 7 letters to spell **enforce**. The police officer was only trying to **enforce** the law.
9. Use 7 letters to spell **perform**. The ballet company was in town to **perform** *The Nutcracker*.
10. Now it's time for the secret word. Take a minute to see if you can figure it out. (After 1 minute, give clues if needed.) Add your letters to **perform** and spell the secret word. The whole cast gave a stunning **performance**.

**Sort:** Display the words on cards in the order they were made, and have each word read aloud. Have the related words sorted. Talk with students about how the words are related, and have students make sentences that combine the related words.

| farm | camp | force | form |
|------|------|-------|------|
| farmer | camper | enforce | reform |
| | | | perform |
| | | | performance |

**Transfer:** Have students use the related words to spell and make sentences for similar words:

close/enclose  large/enlarge  accept/acceptance  assist/assistance

### Word Wall Review—Be a Mind Reader (p. 141)

1. It is in the first half of the alphabet (**A-M**).
2. It does not have a prefix.
3. Bright is not the root word.
4. **Class** is the root word.
5. It has 14 letters.

CD-2420 Big Words for Big Kids © Carson-Dellosa

# Lesson 57

## Letters: e  e  o  d  f  m  r  r
### Words: do  redo  form  free  freed  formed  deform  reform  freedom  reformed

**Make Words:** Distribute the letters and tell students what words to make. After each word is made, show the correct spelling. Make sure everyone has each word spelled correctly before doing the next word. Keep the lesson fast paced.

1. Take 2 letters and spell **do**. What **do** you like to **do**?
2. Add 2 letters and spell **redo**. I lost my homework and had to **redo** it.
3. Use 4 letters to spell **form**. We had to fill out the insurance **form**.
4. Use 4 letters to spell **free**. On Tuesdays, entrance to the museum is **free**.
5. Add a letter to spell **freed**. Abraham Lincoln **freed** the slaves.
6. Use 6 letters to spell **formed**. Four of us got together and **formed** a rock band.
7. Move the letters to spell **deform**. The doctor warned that wearing shoes that are too tight can **deform** the feet.
8. Change 1 letter to spell **reform**. After his arrest, the man promised to **reform**.
9. Use 7 letters to spell **freedom**. Many people fought and died for **freedom**.
10. Now it's time for the secret word. Take a minute to see if you can figure it out. (After 1 minute, give clues if needed.) Add your letters to a word you have already made to spell the secret word. He was put on parole and worked hard, and the judge proclaimed him truly **reformed**.

**Sort:** Display the words on cards in the order they were made, and have each word read aloud. Have the related words sorted. Talk with students about how the words are related, and have students make sentences that combine the related words.

| | | |
|---|---|---|
| do | free | form |
| redo | freed | formed |
| | freedom | deform |
| | | reform |
| | | reformed |

**Transfer:** Have students use the related words to spell and make sentences for similar words:

king/kingdom  bore/boredom  press/depress/repress

## Word Wall Review—Be a Mind Reader (p. 141)

1. It is in the last half of the alphabet (**N-Z**).
2. It has a prefix.
3. It begins with the letter **u**.
4. **Un** is the prefix.
5. It means **the opposite of impressive**.

# Lesson 58

### Letters: e i o d f m r t y
### Words: form edit time dirt dirty timer editor formed deform deformity

**Make Words:** Distribute the letters and tell students what words to make. After each word is made, show the correct spelling. Make sure everyone has each word spelled correctly before doing the next word. Keep the lesson fast paced.

1.  Take 4 letters and spell **form**. We did not know what **form** the retaliation would take.
2.  Use 4 letters to spell **edit**. I need someone to help me **edit** my piece.
3.  Use 4 letters to spell **time**. How much **time** will it take?
4.  Use 4 letters to spell **dirt**. The baby liked to play in the **dirt**.
5.  Add a letter to spell **dirty**. The baby was very **dirty**.
6.  Use 5 letters to spell **timer**. Set the **timer** for 30 minutes.
7.  Use 6 letters to spell **editor**. The **editor** made a lot of changes.
8.  Use 6 letters to spell **formed**. The hurricane **formed** out in the ocean.
9.  Move the letters to spell **deform**. Everyone worried that the injury would **deform** his leg.
10. Now it's time for the secret word. Take a minute to see if you can figure it out. (After 1 minute, give clues if needed.) Add your letters to **deform** to spell the secret word. The leg healed fine, without any **deformity**.

**Sort:** Display the words on cards in the order they were made, and have each word read aloud. Have the related words sorted. Talk with students about how the words are related, and have students make sentences that combine the related words.

| edit | dirt | time | form |
|------|------|------|------|
| editor | dirty | timer | formed |
| | | | deform |
| | | | deformity |

**Transfer:** Have students use the related words to spell and make sentences for similar words:

active/activity   major/majority   minor/minority

### Word Wall Review—Be a Mind Reader (p. 141)

1.  It is in the last half of the alphabet (**N-Z**).
2.  It has a prefix.
3.  It begins with the letter **u**.
4.  **Under** is the prefix.
5.  **Cover** is the root word.

# Lesson 59

## Letters: a e o u f l m r s t
## Words: arm arms form tears formal format armful tearful formula formulates

**Make Words:** Distribute the letters and tell students what words to make. After each word is made, show the correct spelling. Make sure everyone has each word spelled correctly before doing the next word. Keep the lesson fast paced.

1. Take 3 letters and spell **arm**. He broke his **arm**.
2. Add a letter to spell **arms**. Breaking both **arms** would be awful!
3. Use 4 letters to spell **form**. The first step is to **form** the clay with your hands.
4. Use 5 letters to spell **tears**. Everyone was in **tears** at the end of the movie.
5. Use 6 letters to spell **formal**. **Formal** dress was required for the inaugural ball.
6. Change 1 letter to spell **format**. Please help me **format** this document.
7. Use 6 letters to spell **armful**. She came home with an **armful** of packages.
8. Use 7 letters to spell **tearful**. They hugged and said **tearful** good-byes.
9. Use 7 letters to spell **formula**. We bought **formula** for the baby.
10. Now it's time for the secret word. Take a minute to see if you can figure it out. (After 1 minute, give clues if needed.) Add your letters to **formula** to spell the secret word. We will have to wait until the committee **formulates** a plan to solve the problem.

**Sort:** Display the words on cards in the order they were made, and have each word read aloud. Have the related words sorted. Talk with students about how the words are related, and have students make sentences that combine the related words.

| arm | tears | form |
|---|---|---|
| arms | tearful | formal |
| armful | | format |
| | | formula |
| | | formulates |

**Transfer:** Have students use the related words to spell and make sentences for similar words:

**fear/fearful use/useful success/successful**

## Word Wall Review—Be a Mind Reader (p. 141)

1. It is in the first half of the alphabet (**A-M**).
2. It has a prefix.
3. It begins with the letter **d**.
4. It has 10 letters.
5. **Press** is the root word.

# Lesson 60 Word Wall

**Word Wall Words: performance  reformed  deformity  formal  formulates**

Give everyone a copy of the Take-Home Word Wall (p. 163) and/or place the words on the classroom Word Wall:

## Talk about the Words

All these words come from the Latin root **form**, which means form or shape. Have students pronounce each word and tell what prefixes and suffixes have been added. Discuss how the prefixes and suffixes affect the meaning of the words.

**performance:** The root is **form** with the prefix **per** and the suffix **ance**. The prefix **per** sometimes means "through" or "by way of." When you **perform**, you do (verb) something in a certain way or form. **Performance** is the name (noun) for what you do.

**reformed:** The root is **form** with the prefix **re** and the ending **ed**. When you **reform** something, you put it back in better shape. You shape it up.

**deformity:** The root is **form** with the prefix **de** and the suffix **ity**. The prefix **de** often has a negative meaning. Something that is **deformed** is formed wrongly or misshapen. The suffix **ity** often indicates a naming word (noun). The thing that is **deformed** is a **deformity**.

**formal:** The root is **form** with the suffix **al**. Something that is **formal** has to have a particular shape or form.

**formulates:** The root is **form** with the suffix **ate** and the ending **s**. When you **formulate** something, you determine the **form** or shape it will take.

## Cheer for the Words

Lead the class in cheering for each word in a rhythmic way, emphasizing the morphemic parts of the word "**d-e—f-o-r-m—i-t-y**." If possible, cheer for each new word three times.

## Use the Prefixes and Suffixes

Say these sentences aloud, and have students figure out a word with one of the prefixes or suffixes—**de**, **re**, **ity**, **al**, **ance**—that will make sense in the sentence.

- I was **annoyed** when the delivery was late, but I was so happy when it came that I quickly got over my _____.
- The **musicians** played a great variety of different _____ pieces.
- After many years of fighting for **equal** rights, women finally achieved _____.
- The best **offense** is a good _____.
- I **arranged** the office furniture, but my boss didn't like it, so he _____ it.

# Lesson 61

### Letters: e  e  o  p  r  r  r  s  t
### Words: set  pest  post  port  reset  preset  pester  poster  report  reporters

**Make Words:** Distribute the letters and tell students what words to make. After each word is made, show the correct spelling. Make sure everyone has each word spelled correctly before doing the next word. Keep the lesson fast paced.

1. Take 3 letters and spell **set**. We **set** the VCR to record our favorite show.
2. Use 4 letters to spell **pest**. Sometimes, my little brother is a **pest**.
3. Change 1 letter to spell **post**. We will **post** the notice on the message board.
4. Change 1 letter and spell **port**. The ship came into the **port**.
5. Use 5 letters to spell **reset**. When the power came back on, we **reset** all of the clocks.
6. Add a letter to spell **preset**. Everyone met at the **preset** time.
7. Move the letters to spell **pester**. Don't **pester** me!
8. Change 1 letter to spell **poster**. We made a **poster** to hold up at the game.
9. Use 6 letters to spell **report**. My **report** is on killer whales.
10. Now it's time for the secret word. Take a minute to see if you can figure it out. (After 1 minute, give clues if needed.) Add your letters to **report** and spell the secret word. The **reporters** were at the scene of the accident.

**Sort:** Display the words on cards in the order they were made, and have each word read aloud. Have the related words sorted. Talk with students about how the words are related, and have students make sentences that combine the related words.

| set | post | pest | port |
|---|---|---|---|
| reset | poster | pester | report |
| preset | | | reporters |

**Transfer:** Have students use the related words to spell and make sentences for similar words:

**speak/speakers  record/recorders  view/review/preview**

**Word Wall Review—Be a Mind Reader (p. 141)**

1. It is in the first half of the alphabet (**A-M**).
2. It begins with the letter **d**.
3. Dis is not the prefix.
4. **De** is the prefix.
5. It ends with the suffix **ity**.

# Lesson 62

### Letters: a e i o c m n p r t
## Words: act trap port enact entrap import romance romantic reaction importance

**Make Words:** Distribute the letters and tell students what words to make. After each word is made, show the correct spelling. Make sure everyone has each word spelled correctly before doing the next word. Keep the lesson fast paced.

1. Take 3 letters and spell **act**. As the drought got worse, the council had to **act** to protect the community.
2. Use 4 letters and spell **trap**. We set a **trap** to catch the mouse.
3. Use 4 letters to spell **port**. Which **port** does this plug into?
4. Use 5 letters to spell **enact**. The council had to **enact** new laws limiting outdoor watering and car washing.
5. Use 6 letters to spell **entrap**. The FBI had a plan to **entrap** the smugglers.
6. Use 6 letters to spell **import**. We **import** most of our oil from other countries.
7. Use 7 letters to spell **romance**. The movie was a comedy and a **romance**.
8. Use 8 letters to spell **romantic**. I thought the story was very **romantic**.
9. Use 8 letters to spell **reaction**. Not everyone had the same **reaction** to the movie.
10. Now it's time for the secret word. Take a minute to see if you can figure it out. (After 1 minute, give clues if needed.) Add your letters to a word you have already made to spell the secret word. The mayor said he couldn't stress too strongly the **importance** of conserving water.

**Sort:** Display the words on cards in the order they were made, and have each word read aloud. Have the related words sorted. Talk with students about how the words are related, and have students make sentences that combine the related words.

| | | | |
|---|---|---|---|
| act | trap | romance | port |
| enact | entrap | romantic | import |
| reaction | | | importance |

**Transfer:** Have students use the related words to spell and make sentences for similar words:

camp/encamp   force/enforce   circle/encircle   insure/insurance

**Word Wall Review—Be a Mind Reader (p. 141)**

1. It is in the last half of the alphabet (**N-Z**).
2. It has a prefix.
3. **Re** is the prefix.
4. It has 10 letters.
5. It means **appeared again**.

CD-2420 Big Words for Big Kids

# Lesson 63

### Letters: a a i o o n n p r r s t t t
### Words: art port artist nation nations airport patriot patriots transport transportation

**Make Words:** Distribute the letters and tell students what words to make. After each word is made, show the correct spelling. Make sure everyone has each word spelled correctly before doing the next word. Keep the lesson fast paced.

1. Take 3 letters and spell **art**. We hung our **art** in the halls.
2. Use 4 letters to spell **port.** Sailors go to "any **port** in a storm!"
3. Use 6 letters to spell **artist**. The **artist** was painting in the garden.
4. Use 6 letters to spell **nation**. The **nation** called the United States began in 1776.
5. Add a letter to spell **nations**. We visited the United **Nations** in New York City.
6. Use 7 letters to spell **airport**. The **airport** is not far from my house.
7. Use 7 letters to spell **patriot**. A **patriot** is a person who supports the country.
8. Add a letter to spell **patriots**. He was a quarterback with the New England **Patriots**.
9. Use 9 letters to spell **transport**. His job was to **transport** the cars to the car dealers.
10. Now it's time for the secret word. Take a minute to see if you can figure it out. (After 1 minute, give clues if needed.) Add your letters to **transport** to spell the secret word. Cars, trucks, buses, trains, and planes are different kinds of **transportation**.

**Sort:** Display the words on cards in the order they were made, and have each word read aloud. Have the related words sorted. Talk with students about how the words are related, and have students make sentences that combine the related words.

| | | | |
|---|---|---|---|
| art | nation | patriot | port |
| artist | nations | patriots | airport |
| | | | transport |
| | | | transportation |

**Transfer:** Have students use the related words to spell and make sentences for similar words:

### cycle/cyclist  biology/biologist  inform/information  combine/combination

## Word Wall Review—Be a Mind Reader (p. 141)

1. It is in the last half of the alphabet (**N-Z**).
2. It does not have a prefix.
3. Power is not the root word.
4. Sign is not the root word.
5. **Press** is the root word.

# Lesson 64

### Letters: a e e o b l p r t x
### Words: port  pole  polar  export  parole  parolee  operate  operable  portable  exportable

**Make Words:** Distribute the letters and tell students what words to make. After each word is made, show the correct spelling. Make sure everyone has each word spelled correctly before doing the next word. Keep the lesson fast paced.

1. Take 4 letters and spell **port**. The cruise ship docked at the **port**.
2. Use 4 letters to spell **pole**. She traveled to the North **Pole**.
3. Use 5 letters to spell **polar**. She did not see any **polar** bears.
4. Use 6 letters to spell **export**. We **export** computers to many different countries.
5. Use 6 letters to spell **parole**. The man was out on **parole**.
6. Add 1 letter to spell **parolee**. Someone on parole is called a **parolee**.
7. Use 7 letters to spell **operate**. His job was to **operate** the drawbridge.
8. Use 8 letters to spell **operable**. After the flood, the machinery was not in **operable** condition.
9. Use 8 letters to spell **portable**. They brought in **portable** generators.
10. Now it's time for the secret word. Take a minute to see if you can figure it out. (After 1 minute, give clues if needed.) Add your letters to **portable** to spell the secret word. Something you are allowed to export is **exportable**.

**Sort:** Display the words on cards in the order they were made, and have each word read aloud. Have the related words sorted. Talk with students about how the words are related, and have students make sentences that combine the related words.

| pole<br>polar | parole<br>parolee | operate<br>operable | port<br>portable<br>export<br>exportable |
|---|---|---|---|

**Transfer:** Have students use the related words to spell and make sentences for similar words:

### favor/favorable  predict/predictable  comfort/comfortable

## Word Wall Review—Be a Mind Reader (p. 141)

1. It is in the first half of the alphabet (**A-M**).
2. It does not have a prefix.
3. Bright is not the root word.
4. It has 6 letters.
5. **Form** is the root word.

CD-2420 Big Words for Big Kids  © Carson-Dellosa

# Lesson 65 Word Wall

**Word Wall Words: reporters importance transportation portable exportable**

Give everyone a copy of the Take-Home Word Wall (p. 164) and/or place the words on the classroom Word Wall.

## Talk about the Words

All of these words come from the Latin root **port**, which means "carry" or "bring." Have students pronounce each word and tell what prefixes and suffixes have been added. Discuss how the prefixes and suffixes affect the meaning of the words.

**reporters:** The root is **port** with the prefix **re**, the suffix **er**, and the **s** ending. The prefix **re** sometimes means "back" or "again." When you **report**, you bring back the story. **Reporters** are people who **report**.

**importance:** The root is **port** with the prefix **im** and the suffix **ance**. The prefix **im** sometimes means "in." When you bring something in, you **import** it. Presumably, the things you bring in are worth carrying back and thus have **importance**.

**transportation:** The root is **port** with the prefix **trans** and the suffix **tion**. The prefix **trans** sometimes means "across." When you **transport** things across the country, you bring them across the country. The system of transporting things is called **transportation**.

**portable:** The root is **port** with the suffix **able**. Something that is **portable** is **able** to be carried.

**exportable:** The root is **port** with the prefix **ex** and the suffix **able**. The prefix **ex** often means "out." When you send things out of the country, you **export** them. Something that is **exportable** is **able** to be **exported**.

## Cheer for the Words

Lead the class in cheering for each word in a rhythmic way, emphasizing the morphemic parts of the word "**e-x—p-o-r-t—a-b-l-e**." If possible, cheer for each new word three times.

## Use the Prefixes and Suffixes

Say these sentences aloud, and have students figure out a word with one of the prefixes or suffixes—**trans**, **ex**, **re**, **im**, **able**, **ance**—that will make sense in the sentence.

* The woman **depends** on her children to care for her. Fortunately, all of her children are very

  _____.
* They **assist** her in lots of tasks, and she is grateful for their _____.
* They painted all the **interior** walls and now they are getting ready to paint the

  _____.
* The maximum security **prison** was full of men who had been _____ most of their adult lives.
* These **plants** need more sun, so I am going to _____ them in a sunnier part of the garden.
* I got a phone **call** telling me that my truck had been _____ because of a defect in the brakes.

# Lesson 66

**Letters:** e i i o c d n p r s t
**Words:** port deport direct predict inspect indirect conspire conspired inspector directions predictions

**Make Words:** Distribute the letters and tell students what words to make. After each word is made, show the correct spelling. Make sure everyone has each word spelled correctly before doing the next word. Keep the lesson fast paced.

1. Take 4 letters and spell **port**. He tried to enter the **port** without the proper papers.
2. Add 2 letters to spell **deport**. The immigration officials decided to **deport** him.
3. Use 6 letters to spell **direct**. Could you **direct** me to the shopping mall?
4. Use 7 letters and spell **predict**. What do you **predict** will happen?
5. Use 7 letters to spell **inspect**. The buyers came to **inspect** the property.
6. Use 8 letters to spell **indirect**. We got here late because we took a rather **indirect** route.
7. Use 8 letters to spell **conspire**. When you **conspire**, you plan in secrecy.
8. Add a letter to spell **conspired**. His friends **conspired** to surprise him on his birthday.
9. Use 9 letters to spell **inspector**. The **inspector** arrived and began collecting evidence.
10. Use 10 letters to spell **directions**. She gave me bad **directions**, and I got lost.
11. Now it's time for the secret word. Take a minute to see if you can figure it out. (After 1 minute, give clues if needed.) Add your letters to a word you have already made and spell the secret word. Her **predictions** turned out to be true.

**Sort:** Display the words on cards in the order they were made, and have each word read aloud. Have the related words sorted. Talk with students about how the words are related, and have students make sentences that combine the related words.

| port | direct | conspire | inspect | predict |
| deport | indirect | conspired | inspector | predictions |
|  | directions |  |  |  |

**Transfer:** Have students use the related words to spell and make sentences for similar words:

director  inspection  collect/collector/collection  exhibit/exhibitor/exhibition

**Word Wall Review—Be a Mind Reader (p. 141)**

1. It is in the middle section of the alphabet (**I-Q**).
2. It has 10 letters.
3. Power is not the root.
4. It does not have a prefix.
5. It ends with the suffix **ship**.

# Lesson 67

## Letters: a e e i u b c d l n p r t
**Words: build alter center central altered rebuild predict unaltered predictable unpredictable**

**Make Words:** Distribute the letters and tell students what words to make. After each word is made, show the correct spelling. Make sure everyone has each word spelled correctly before doing the next word. Keep the lesson fast paced.

1. Take 5 letters and spell **build**. We are going to **build** a treehouse.
2. Use 5 letters and spell **alter**. It rained all weekend so we had to **alter** our plans.
3. Use 6 letters to spell **center**. The bank is located in the **center** of the city.
4. Use 7 letters to spell **central**. A **central** location is good for business.
5. Use 7 letters to spell **altered**. We **altered** our plan to fit his schedule.
6. Use 7 letters to spell **rebuild**. After the storm, we had to **rebuild** our treehouse.
7. Use 7 letters to spell **predict**. I **predict** we are going to have lots of snow this winter.
8. Use 9 letters to spell **unaltered**. The opposite of altered is **unaltered**.
9. Use 11 letters to spell **predictable**. Her behavior was very **predictable**.
10. Now it's time for the secret word. Take a minute to see if you can figure it out. (After 1 minute, give clues if needed.) Add your letters to **predictable** to spell the secret word. The weather was very **unpredictable**.

**Sort:** Display the words on cards in the order they were made, and have each word read aloud. Have the related words sorted. Talk with students about how the words are related, and have students make sentences that combine the related words.

| build | center | alter | predict |
|-------|--------|-------|---------|
| rebuild | central | altered | predictable |
|  |  | unaltered | unpredictable |

**Transfer:** Have students use the related words to spell and make sentences for similar words:

believe/believable/unbelievable   reason/reasonable/unreasonable   rely/reliable/unreliable

**Word Wall Review—Be a Mind Reader (p. 141)**

1. It is in the middle section of the alphabet (**I-Q**).
2. It has a prefix and a suffix.
3. It begins with **i**.
4. Inter is not the prefix.
5. The suffix is **ance**.

# Lesson 68

## Letters: a  i  i  o  o  c  c  d  n  n  r  s  t  t
### Words: act donors distract distraction cartoons donation contracts cartoonist contradict contraction contradictions

**Make Words:** Distribute the letters and tell students what words to make. After each word is made, show the correct spelling. Make sure everyone has each word spelled correctly before doing the next word. Keep the lesson fast paced.

1. Take 3 letters and spell **act**. Don't put on an **act**!
2. Use 6 letters to spell **donors**. The **donors** gave millions of dollars to the campaign.
3. Use 8 letters to spell **distract**. I'll **distract** him while you sneak in with his gift.
4. Use 8 letters to spell **cartoons**. Do you like to watch **cartoons**?
5. Use 8 letters to spell **donation**. We gave a **donation** to the Red Cross.
6. Use 9 letters to spell **contracts**. When something **contracts**, it gets smaller.
7. Use 10 letters to spell **cartoonist**. A **cartoonist** creates cartoons.
8. Use 10 letters to spell **contradict**. I don't want to **contradict** you, but that is not the way the accident happened.
9. Use 11 letters to spell **distraction**. The television is a real **distraction** when I'm trying to study.
10. Change 3 letters to spell **contraction**. "Can't" is a **contraction**.
11. Now it's time for the secret word. Take a minute to see if you can figure it out. (After 1 minute, give clues if needed.) Add your letters to a word you have already made to spell the secret word. The judge invited both attorneys into his chambers and attempted to clear up the **contradictions**.

**Sort:** Display the words on cards in the order they were made, and have each word read aloud. Have the related words sorted. Talk with students about how the words are related, and have students make sentences that combine the related words.

| act | cartoons | donors | contracts | contradict |
| distract | cartoonist | donation | contraction | contradictions |
| distraction | | | | |

**Transfer:** Have students use the related words to spell and make sentences for similar words:

invent/invention  construct/construction  subtract/subtraction

**Word Wall Review—Be a Mind Reader (p. 141)**

1. It is in the last section of the alphabet (**R-Z**).
2. **Re** is the prefix.
3. It has an **o**.
4. The suffix is not tion.
5. **Port** is the root word.

# Lesson 69

## Letters: a i i o c d h p r s t t
## Words: art taco tacos artist artistic dictator patriots patriotic dictators dictatorship

**Make Words:** Distribute the letters and tell students what words to make. After each word is made, show the correct spelling. Make sure everyone has each word spelled correctly before doing the next word. Keep the lesson fast paced.

1. Take 3 letters and spell **art**. <u>We are going to the **art** exhibit.</u>
2. Use 4 letters to spell **taco**. <u>Have you ever had a fish **taco**?</u>
3. Add a letter to spell **tacos**. <u>Almost everyone likes **tacos**.</u>
4. Use 6 letters to spell **artist**. <u>The **artist** painted portraits of famous people.</u>
5. Add 2 letters to spell **artistic**. <u>Some people are just naturally **artistic**.</u>
6. Use 8 letters to spell **dictator**. <u>Hitler was a **dictator**.</u>
7. Use 8 letters to spell **patriots**. <u>The **patriots** waved flags as the parade came down the street.</u>
8. Use 9 letters to spell **patriotic**. <u>The 4<sup>th</sup> of July is a **patriotic** holiday in the United States.</u>
9. Use 9 letters to spell **dictators**. <u>Many countries are ruled by **dictators**.</u>
10. Now it's time for the secret word. Take a minute to see if you can figure it out. (After 1 minute, give clues if needed.) Add your letters to **dictators** to spell the secret word. <u>After the revolution, the **dictatorship** was replaced with a democratic government.</u>

**Sort:** Display the words on cards in the order they were made, and have each word read aloud. Have the related words sorted. Talk with students about how the words are related, and have students make sentences that combine the related words.

| | | | |
|---|---|---|---|
| taco | art | patriots | dictator |
| tacos | artist | patriotic | dictators |
| | artistic | | dictatorship |

**Transfer:** Have students use the related words to spell and make sentences for similar words:

**rhythm/rhythmic   graph/graphic   scene/scenic**

## Word Wall Review—Be a Mind Reader (p. 141)

1. It is in the first section of the alphabet (**A-H**).
2. It does not have a prefix.
3. **Bright** is the root word.
4. It does not have an s.
5. The suffix is **ness**.

## Lesson 70  Word Wall

**Word Wall Words: predictions  unpredictable  contradictions  dictator  dictatorship**

Give everyone a copy of the Take-Home Word Wall (p. 165) and/or place the words on the classroom Word Wall.

## Talk about the Words

All these words come from the Latin root **dic**, which means "say" or "speak." **Diction** is speech. You look up all the words you can say and their pronunciations in the **dictionary**. Have students pronounce each word and tell what prefixes and suffixes have been added. Discuss how the prefixes and suffixes affect the meaning of the words.

**predictions:** The root is **dic** with the prefix **pre**, the suffix **tion**, and the **s** ending. The prefix **pre** sometimes means "before" or "earlier." When you **predict** something, you say what will happen before it happens. **Predictions** are what you have when you **predict**.

**unpredictable:** The root is **dic** with the prefixes **un** and **pre** and the suffix **able**. Something **predictable** can be **predicted** . It is **able** to be **predicted**. **Unpredictable** is the opposite of **predictable**.

**contradictions:** The root is **dic** with the prefix **contra**, the suffix **tion**, and the **s** ending. The prefix **contra** sometimes means "against" or "opposite." When you **contradict** something, you speak against it or express an opposite view. **Contradictions** are what you have when you **contradict**.

**dictators:** The root is **dic** with the suffix **or** and the **s** ending. **Dictators** are people who insist on telling everyone else what to do! Their word is law!

**dictatorship:** The root is **dic** with the suffixes **or** and **ship**. **Ship** generally indicates a shared quality. **Dictators** don't share power in their governments, but the kind of governments common to all **dictators** is called **dictatorship**. Other Word Wall words with **ship** as a suffix are **leadership** and **dealership**.

## Cheer for the Words

Lead the class in cheering for each word in a rhythmic way, emphasizing the morphemic parts of the word "**c-o-n-t-r-a—d-i-c—t-i-o-n-s**." If possible, cheer for each new word three times.

## Use the Prefixes and Suffixes

Say these sentences aloud, and have students figure out a word with one of the prefixes or suffixes—**un, pre, ship, able, tion**—that will make sense in the sentence.

- I like to **imagine** things, and everyone says I have a great _____.
- Although everyone knew I **owned** the bike, the police would not return it to me until I could provide proof of _____.
- Our team was **unbeaten** until the tournament, and everyone thought they were _____.
- The movie was supposed to be **exciting**, but I almost fell asleep it was so _____.
- My little brother isn't old enough for **school** yet, so he goes to _____.

# Lesson 71

### Letters: e i i o m n p r s s
**Words:** rise  risen  press  promise  impress  mission  emission  promises  impression  permission

**Make Words:** Distribute the letters and tell students what words to make. After each word is made, show the correct spelling. Make sure everyone has each word spelled correctly before doing the next word. Keep the lesson fast paced.

1. Take 4 letters and spell **rise**. The sun will **rise** at 6:00 A.M.
2. Add a letter to spell **risen**. The sun has **risen**.
3. Use 5 letters to spell **press**. **Press** the button.
4. Use 7 letters and spell **promise**. I made a **promise** to be home early.
5. Use 7 letters to spell **impress**. I dressed up to **impress** the visitors.
6. Use 7 letters to spell **mission**. They sent us on a **mission**.
7. Add a letter to spell **emission**. Our state has strict **emission** controls for cars.
8. Use 8 letters to spell **promises**. He broke all of his **promises**.
9. Today there are 2 secret words. Add your letters to two words we have already made to spell the secret words. (Let students try to figure them out.) I got his **permission** to take the job. I made a good **impression** in my job interview.

**Sort:** Display the words on cards in the order they were made, and have each word read aloud. Have the related words sorted. Talk with students about how the words are related, and have students make sentences that combine the related words.

| | | |
|---|---|---|
| rise | press | promise |
| risen | impress | promises |
| | impression | mission |
| | | emission |
| | | permission |

**Transfer:** Have students use the related words to spell and make sentences for similar words:

depress/depression  confess/confession  admit/admission

**Word Wall Review—Be a Mind Reader (p. 141)**

1. It is in the last section of the alphabet (**R-Z**).
2. It begins with the prefix **un**.
3. Health is not the root word.
4. Dic is not the root.
5. It means **the opposite of impressive**.

# Lesson 72

### Letters: a e i d m n r s t t t
**Words:** train admit remit treat treats trained readmit mistreat transmit transmitted

**Make Words:** Distribute the letters and tell students what words to make. After each word is made, show the correct spelling. Make sure everyone has each word spelled correctly before doing the next word. Keep the lesson fast paced.

1.  Take 5 letters and spell **train**. <u>I am going to **train** for the job.</u>
2.  Use 5 letters and spell **admit**. <u>I had to **admit** that I made a mistake.</u>
3.  Change 2 letters to spell **remit**. <u>The letter said I had to **remit** the payment immediately.</u>
4.  Use 5 letters to spell **treat**. <u>My cousin does not **treat** his dog very well.</u>
5.  Add a letter to spell **treats.** <u>The cardiologist **treats** people with heart problems.</u>
6.  Use 7 letters to spell **trained**. <u>I **trained** my dog to roll over.</u>
7.  Use 7 letters to spell **readmit**. <u>She had a relapse after leaving the hospital and they had to **readmit** her.</u>
8.  Use 8 letters to spell **mistreat**. <u>I don't understand how anyone can **mistreat** an animal.</u>
9.  Use 8 letters to spell **transmit**. <u>She said she would **transmit** the message.</u>
10. Now it's time for the secret word. Take a minute to see if you can figure it out. (After 1 minute, give clues if needed.) Add your letters to **transmit** to spell the secret word. <u>She **transmitted** the message via E-mail.</u>

**Sort:** Display the words on cards in the order they were made, and have each word read aloud. Have the related words sorted. Talk with students about how the words are related, and have students make sentences that combine the related words.

| | | |
|---|---|---|
| treat | train | remit |
| treats | trained | admit |
| mistreat | | readmit |
| | | transmit |
| | | transmitted |

**Transfer:** Have students use the related words to spell and make sentences for similar words:

form/transform/transformed   remit/remitted   admit/admitted   permit/permitted

## Word Wall Review—Be a Mind Reader (p. 141)

1.  It is in the middle section of the alphabet (**I-Q**).
2.  It begins with **p**.
3.  Power is not the root word.
4.  It has a prefix and a suffix.
5.  **Dic** is the root.

CD-2420 *Big Words for Big Kids*          © Carson-Dellosa

# Lesson 73

### Letters: e o o c m p r s s
**Words:** pose rose come poem poems roses comes press compose compress composers

**Make Words:** Distribute the letters and tell students what words to make. After each word is made, show the correct spelling. Make sure everyone has each word spelled correctly before doing the next word. Keep the lesson fast paced.

1. Take 4 letters and spell **pose**. We all had to **pose** for the family photo.
2. Change 1 letter to spell **rose**. She picked a yellow **rose**.
3. Use 4 letters to spell **come**. I hope my dog will **come** home.
4. Use 4 letters to spell **poem**. Do you want me to read my **poem**?
5. Add a letter to spell **poems**. I am going to write a book of **poems**.
6. Use 5 letters to spell **roses**. He gave her as dozen red **roses** on Valentine's Day.
7. Use 5 letters to spell **comes**. The mail **comes** around 3:00.
8. Use 5 letters to spell **press**. I am going to **press** him to give me a final decision.
9. Use 7 letters to spell **compose**. I am trying to **compose** a persuasive letter.
10. Use 8 letters to spell **compress**. When you **compress** something, you make it smaller.
11. Now it's time for the secret word. Take a minute to see if you can figure it out. (After 1 minute, give clues if needed.) Add your letters to a word you have already made to spell the secret word. Bach, Beethoven, and Mozart are famous **composers**.

**Sort:** Display the words on cards in the order they were made, and have each word read aloud. Have the related words sorted. Talk with students about how the words are related, and have students make sentences that combine the related words.

| | | | | |
|---|---|---|---|---|
| rose | come | press | poem | pose |
| roses | comes | compress | poems | compose |
| | | | | composers |

**Transfer:** Have students use the related words to spell and make sentences for similar words:

compute/computer   command/commander   commute/commuter

**Word Wall Review—Be a Mind Reader (p. 141)**

1. It is in the first section of the alphabet (**A-H**).
2. It begins with the letter **c**.
3. Create is not the root word.
4. Class is not the root word.
5. It ends with **ly**.

**Letters: i i i o b l m p s s t y**
**Words: oil oily boss omit omits bossy possibly impossibly possibility impossibility**

**Make Words:** Distribute the letters and tell students what words to make. After each word is made, show the correct spelling. Make sure everyone has each word spelled correctly before doing the next word. Keep the lesson fast paced.

1. Take 3 letters and spell **oil**. The truck leaked **oil**.
2. Add a letter to spell **oily.** There was a big **oily** spot in my driveway.
3. Use 4 letters to spell **boss**. I want to be the **boss**.
4. Use 4 letters to spell **omit**. It was a mistake to **omit** my name from the list.
5. Add a letter to spell **omits**. She makes mistakes and **omits** names all of the time.
6. Use 5 letters to spell **bossy**. People don't like him because he is so **bossy**.
7. Use 8 letters to spell **possibly**. Come if you **possibly** can.
8. Add 2 letters to spell **impossibly**. Today was **impossibly** busy.
9. Use 11 letters to spell **possibility**. There was a good **possibility** that they would make it to the top of the mountain.
10. Now it's time for the secret word. Take a minute to see if you can figure it out. (After 1 minute, give clues if needed.) Add your letters to **possibility** to spell the secret word. Making it to the top of Mt. Everest was an **impossibility**.

**Sort:** Display the words on cards in the order they were made, and have each word read aloud. Have the related words sorted. Talk with students about how the words are related, and have students make sentences that combine the related words.

| oil | boss | omit | possibly |
|-----|------|------|----------|
| oily | bossy | omits | impossibly |
| | | | possibility |
| | | | impossibility |

**Transfer:** Have students use the related words to spell and make sentences for similar words:

major/majority  minor/minority  active/activity

**Word Wall Review—Be a Mind Reader (p. 141)**

1. It is in the first section of the alphabet (**A-H**).
2. It begins with the letter **c**.
3. Create is not the root word.
4. Class is not the root word.
5. **Contra** is the prefix.

Give everyone a copy of the Take-Home Word Wall (p. 166) and/or place the words on the classroom Word Wall.

## Talk about the Words

All of these words come from the Latin root **mis** or **mit**, which means "send" or **pos** which means "put" or "place." A **mission** is something you are sent on. Your **position** is where you put yourself. Discuss these words and how the prefixes and suffixes affect the meaning.

**permission:** The root is **mis** with the prefix **per** and the suffix **sion**. The prefix **per** sometimes means "through." **Permission** is what you need to send you through to where you need to go.

**transmitted:** The root is **mit** with the prefix **trans** and the ending **ed**. The prefix **trans** sometimes means "across." When something is **transmitted**, it is sent across from one place to another.

**emission:** The root is **mis** with the prefix **e** and the suffix **sion**. The prefix **e (ex)** sometimes means "out." An **emission** is something that is sent out.

**composers:** The root is **pos** with the prefix **com**, the suffix **or**, and the **s** ending. **Com** sometimes means "with" or "together." **Composers** combine things and put things together.

**impossibility:** The root is **pos** with the prefix **im** and the suffixes **ible** and **ity**. **A possibility** is something that is able to be put into place. **Impossibility** is the opposite of **possibility**.

## Cheer for the Words

Lead the class in cheering for each word in a rhythmic way, emphasizing the morphemic parts of the word "**i-m—p-o-s—s-i-b-i-l—i-t-y**." If possible, cheer for each new word three times.

## Use the Prefixes and Suffixes

Say these sentences aloud, and have students figure out a word with one of the prefixes or suffixes—**im**, **e**, **com**, **per**, **trans**, **ity**, **sion**—that will make sense in the sentence.

- A flight that goes across the **continent** is a _____ flight.
- We all **discussed** the new laws and had a very heated _____.
- Making older people financially **secure** is the goal of Social _____.
- There was a lot of **motion** on one end of the field, and we went over to see what all the _____ was about.
- A long line **formed** to get tickets for the final _____ of the rock group.
- Our request to protest was **rejected**, and we were all _____ from the park.

# Lesson 76

### Letters: e e i o n n p r t v
### Words: open  vote  voter  prove  proven  opener  invent  prevent  inventor  prevention

**Make Words:** Distribute the letters and tell students what words to make. After each word is made, show the correct spelling. Make sure everyone has each word spelled correctly before doing the next word. Keep the lesson fast paced.

1. Take 4 letters and spell **open**. <u>**Open** the windows.</u>
2. Use 4 letters to spell **vote**. <u>We will **vote** on Tuesday.</u>
3. Add a letter to spell **voter**. <u>A person who votes is a **voter**.</u>
4. Use 5 letters and spell **prove**. <u>The prosecutor has to **prove** the defendant is guilty.</u>
5. Add a letter to spell **proven**. <u>A defendant is innocent until **proven** guilty.</u>
6. Use 6 letters to spell **opener**. <u>We got a new garage door **opener**.</u>
7. Use 6 letters to spell **invent**. <u>It is fun to **invent** new games.</u>
8. Use 7 letters to spell **prevent**. <u>Our neighborhood watch group tries to **prevent** crimes.</u>
9. Use 8 letters to spell **inventor**. <u>Thomas Edison was a famous **inventor**.</u>
10. Now it's time for the secret word. Take a minute to see if you can figure it out. (After 1 minute, give clues if needed.) Add your letters to a word we have already made to spell the secret word. <u>An ounce of **prevention** is worth a pound of cure!</u>

**Sort:** Display the words on cards in the order they were made, and have each word read aloud. Have the related words sorted. Talk with students about how the words are related, and have students make sentences that combine the related words.

| vote | prove | open | invent |
|------|-------|------|--------|
| voter | proven | opener | inventor |
| | | | prevent |
| | | | prevention |

**Transfer:** Have students use the related words to spell and make sentences for similar words:

give/given  broke/broken  froze/frozen  take/taken

**Word Wall Review—Be a Mind Reader (p. 141)**

1. It is in the last section of the alphabet (**R-Z**).
2. It has 11 letters.
3. Sign is not the root word.
4. It begins with the suffix **trans**.
5. It means **sent across from one place to another.**

# Lesson 77

**Letters:** e e i i o n n r t t v
**Words:** net rot vote voter event invent rotten Internet inventor invention intervention

**Make Words:** Distribute the letters and tell students what words to make. After each word is made, show the correct spelling. Make sure everyone has each word spelled correctly before doing the next word. Keep the lesson fast paced.

1. Take 3 letters and spell **net**. He hit the ball into the **net**.
2. Use 3 letters and spell **rot**. Too much rain will **rot** the fruit.
3. Use 4 letters to spell **vote**. Who are you going to **vote** for?
4. Add a letter to spell **voter**. The **voter** turnout was very low.
5. Use 5 letters to spell **event**. The wedding was a glorious **event**.
6. Use 6 letters to spell **invent**. What would you like to **invent**?
7. Use 6 letters to spell **rotten**. The power was off for a week, and all of the food in Jennifer's refrigerator was **rotten**.
8. Use 8 letters to spell **Internet**. You can travel the world on the **Internet**.
9. Use 8 letters to spell **inventor**. Alexander Graham Bell was the **inventor** of the telephone.
10. Use 9 letters to spell **invention**. The telephone was a great **invention**.
11. Now it's time for the secret word. Take a minute to see if you can figure it out. (After 1 minute, give clues if needed.) The secret word begins with the prefix **inter**. The small country sought our **intervention** to stop the civil war.

**Sort:** Display the words on cards in the order they were made, and have each word read aloud. Have the related words sorted. Talk with students about how the words are related, and have students make sentences that combine the related words. (The Latin root **ven** means **come**. An event is something people come to. An inventor is someone who comes up with things.)

| vote | rot | net | event |
|------|-----|-----|-------|
| voter | rotten | Internet | invent |
| | | | inventor |
| | | | invention |
| | | | intervention |

**Transfer:** Have students use the related words to spell and make sentences for similar words:

got/gotten   forgot/forgotten   flat/flatten   write/written

## Word Wall Review—Be a Mind Reader (p. 141)

1. It is in the middle section of the alphabet (**I-Q**).
2. It begins with **p**.
3. It has a prefix and a suffix.
4. Form is not the root.
5. It ends with the suffix **sion**.

# Lesson 78

### Letters: e i o c n p r s s t
**Words:** post poster prince copies copier inspect princess conspire conspires inspectors

**Make Words:** Distribute the letters and tell students what words to make. After each word is made, show the correct spelling. Make sure everyone has each word spelled correctly before doing the next word. Keep the lesson fast paced.

1. Take 4 letters and spell **post**. We stopped at the **post** office.
2. Add 2 letters to spell **poster**. His picture was on a "wanted" **poster**.
3. Use 6 letters to spell **prince**. The frog turned into a **prince**.
4. Use 6 letters to spell **copies**. I need to make 100 **copies**.
5. Change 1 letter to spell **copier**. The **copier** was broken.
6. Use 7 letters to spell **inspect**. The general came to **inspect** the troops.
7. Use 8 letters to spell **princess**. Cinderella married the prince and became a **princess**.
8. Use 8 letters to spell **conspire**. Let's **conspire** to play a trick on them.
9. Add a letter to spell **conspires**. The teacher **conspires** with the students to plan the trick.
10. Now it's time for the secret word. Take a minute to see if you can figure it out. (After 1 minute, give clues if needed.) Add your letters to a word you have already made to spell the secret word. The **inspectors** made a surprise visit to the factory.

**Sort:** Display the words on cards in the order they were made, and have each word read aloud. Have the related words sorted. Talk with students about how the words are related, and have students make sentences that combine the related words.

| post | copies | prince | conspire | inspect |
|------|--------|--------|----------|---------|
| poster | copier | princess | conspires | inspectors |

**Transfer:** Have students use the related words to spell and make sentences for similar words:

act/actress   host/hostess   wait/waitress   count/countess

## Word Wall Review—Be a Mind Reader (p. 141)

1. It is in the first section of the alphabet (**A-H**).
2. It begins with the letter **e**.
3. Courage is not the root word.
4. It ends with the suffix **sion**.
5. It means **something sent out**.

# Lesson 79

## Letters: a e o c p r s s t t
## Words: act actor react toast coast coaster toaster actress spectator spectators

**Make Words:** Distribute the letters and tell students what words to make. After each word is made, show the correct spelling. Make sure everyone has each word spelled correctly before doing the next word. Keep the lesson fast paced.

1. Take 3 letters and spell **act**. Don't **act** like a fool!
2. Add 2 letters to spell **actor**. He was a famous **actor**.
3. Use 5 letters to spell **react**. In an emergency, we have to **react** immediately.
4. Use 5 letters to spell **toast**. I like **toast** and peanut butter.
5. Change a letter to spell **coast**. We pedal uphill and **coast** downhill.
6. Add 2 letters to spell **coaster**. Did you ever ride a roller **coaster**?
7. Change 1 letter to spell **toaster**. You can toast things in a **toaster**.
8. Use 7 letters to spell **actress**. She was a famous **actress**.
9. Use 9 letters to spell **spectator**. I wish I were a baseball player, but I am only a **spectator**.
10. Now it's time for the secret word. Take a minute to see if you can figure it out. (After 1 minute, give clues if needed.) Add your letters to **spectator** to spell the secret word. The **spectators** at the Olympics were awed by the talents of the athletes.

**Sort:** Display the words on cards in the order they were made, and have each word read aloud. Have the related words sorted. Talk with students about how the words are related, and have students make sentences that combine the related words.

| | | | |
|---|---|---|---|
| act | coast | toast | spectator |
| actor | coaster | toaster | spectators |
| react | | | |
| actress | | | |

**Transfer:** Have students use the related words to spell and make sentences for similar words:

box/boxer  kick/kicker  catch/catcher  pitch/pitcher

## Word Wall Review—Be a Mind Reader (p. 141)

1. It is in the first section of the alphabet (**A-H**).
2. It begins with the letter **e**.
3. Courage is not the root word.
4. It begins with the prefix **ex**.
5. It means **able to be exported**.

Give everyone a copy of the Take-Home Word Wall (p. 167) and/or place the words on the classroom Word Wall.

## Talk about the Words

All these words come from the Latin root **ven**, which means "come," or **spec**, which means "look" or "watch." A **venue** is a place people come to. Something **spectacular** is amazing to watch. Discuss these words and how the prefixes and suffixes affect the meaning.

**prevention:** The root is **ven** with the prefix **pre** and the suffix **tion**. The prefix **pre** sometimes means "before" or "earlier." When you **prevent** something, you take action to avoid something before it comes.

**intervention:** The root is **ven** with the prefix **inter** and the suffix **tion**. The prefix **inter** means "between" or "within." When you **intervene**, you do something to come between the groups in conflict.

**inventor:** The root is **ven** with the prefix **in** and the suffix **or**. An **inventor** comes up with new things or makes improvements in old things.

**inspectors:** The root is **spec** with the prefix **in**, the suffix **or**, and the **s** ending. **Inspectors** are people who look into what is happening.

**spectators:** The root is **spec** with the suffix **or** and the **s** ending. **Spectators** are people who watch the action.

## Cheer for the Words

Lead the class in cheering for each word in a rhythmic way, emphasizing the morphemic parts of the word "i-n—s-p-e-c-t—o-r-s." If possible, cheer for each new word three times.

## Use the Prefixes and Suffixes

Say these sentences aloud, and have students figure out a word with one of the prefixes or suffixes—**pre, in, inter, or, tion**—that will make sense in the sentence.

- We got to the **game** early so we could watch the _____ show.
- We all **contributed** to make the show a success, but the dancers made the most important _____.
- The person who **directs** the show is called the _____.
- He used to be an **outfielder**, but now he's an _____.
- The most dangerous **section** of this road is the _____ of five streets.

# Lesson 81

**Letters: e e i i o l n s t v**
**Words: vote live liven votes novel stole stolen vision novelist television**

**Make Words:** Distribute the letters and tell students what words to make. After each word is made, show the correct spelling. Make sure everyone has each word spelled correctly before doing the next word. Keep the lesson fast paced.

1. Take 4 letters and spell **vote**. Every **vote** counts!
2. Use 4 letters to spell **live**. The show was broadcast **live**.
3. Add a letter to spell **liven**. We need to **liven** up this party.
4. Use 5 letters and spell **votes**. The winner is the one who gets the most **votes**.
5. Use 5 letters to spell **novel**. Her first **novel** became a best seller.
6. Use 5 letters to spell **stole**. Someone **stole** my bike.
7. Add a letter to spell **stolen**. It was **stolen** out of our garage.
8. Use 7 letters to spell **vision**. I have 20/20 **vision**.
9. Use 8 letters to spell **novelist**. A **novelist** is a person who writes novels.
10. Now it's time for the secret word. Take a minute to see if you can figure it out. (After 1 minute, give clues if needed.) Add your letters to a word we have already made to spell the secret word. I like to watch **television**.

**Sort:** Display the words on cards in the order they were made, and have each word read aloud. Have the related words sorted. Talk with students about how the words are related, and have students make sentences that combine the related words.

| vote | novel | live | stole | vision |
|------|-------|------|-------|--------|
| votes | novelist | liven | stolen | television |

**Transfer:** Have students use the related words to spell and make sentences for similar words:

**drive/driven  rise/risen  phone/telephone  scope/telescope**

**Word Wall Review—Be a Mind Reader (p. 141)**

1. It is in the last section of the alphabet (**R-Z**).
2. Re is not the prefix.
3. Un is not the prefix.
4. It has 10 letters.
5. It means **people who watch an event**.

# Lesson 82

### Letters: e i i o u n p r s s v
### Words: virus prove proves proven visors vision viruses inspire inspires supervision

**Make Words:** Distribute the letters and tell students what words to make. After each word is made, show the correct spelling. Make sure everyone has each word spelled correctly before doing the next word. Keep the lesson fast paced.

1. Take 5 letters and spell **virus**. A cold is caused by a **virus**.
2. Use 5 letters and spell **prove**. The detective gathered evidence to **prove** his case.
3. Add a letter to spell **proves**. He **proves** she could not have committed the crime.
4. Change a letter to spell **proven**. Once her innocence was **proven**, she was released.
5. Use 6 letters to spell **visors**. The golfers all wore **visors** so they could see in the sun.
6. Use 6 letters to spell **vision**. Good **vision** is very important for golfers.
7. Use 7 letters to spell **viruses**. **Viruses** cause many different diseases.
8. Use 7 letters to spell **inspire**. A beautiful sunset can **inspire** a painter.
9. Add a letter to spell **inspires**. What **inspires** you?
10. Now it's time for the secret word. Take a minute to see if you can figure it out. (After 1 minute, give clues if needed.) Add your letters to a word you have already made to spell the secret word. The nurses worked under the **supervision** of the doctors.

**Sort:** Display the words on cards in the order they were made, and have each word read aloud. Have the related words sorted. Talk with students about how the words are related, and have students make sentences that combine the related words. (The Latin root **vis** means "see." Visors help you see by shading the sun. When you supervise, you oversee something.)

| | | | |
|---|---|---|---|
| prove | virus | inspire | visors |
| proves | viruses | inspires | vision |
| proven | | | supervision |

**Transfer:** Have students use the related words to spell and make sentences for similar words:

**man/superman human/superhuman sonic/supersonic natural/supernatural**

### Word Wall Review—Be a Mind Reader (p. 141)

1. It is in the first section of the alphabet (**A-H**).
2. It has 9 letters.
3. Health is not the root.
4. Bright is not the root.
5. **Act** is the root.

# Lesson 83

## Letters: a i o u b c n r s t t
## Words: art tour tours artist tourist botanic botanist traction subtract subtraction

**Make Words:** Distribute the letters and tell students what words to make. After each word is made, show the correct spelling. Make sure everyone has each word spelled correctly before doing the next word. Keep the lesson fast paced.

1. Take 3 letters and spell **art**. <u>I am taking an **art** class.</u>
2. Use 4 letters to spell **tour**. <u>She has a summer job as a **tour** guide.</u>
3. Add a letter to spell **tours**. <u>She does several **tours** each day.</u>
4. Use 6 letters to spell **artist**. <u>The art class is taught by a local **artist**.</u>
5. Use 7 letters to spell **tourist**. <u>The lost **tourist** stopped and asked for directions.</u>
6. Use 7 letters to spell **botanic**. <u>They took a tour of the **botanic** gardens.</u>
7. Use 8 letters to spell **botanist**. <u>A **botanist** studies plants.</u>
8. Use 8 letters to spell **traction**. <u>We were slipping because we couldn't get any **traction** on the icy roads.</u>
9. Use 8 letters to spell **subtract**. <u>My brother is learning to add and **subtract**.</u>
10. Now it's time for the secret word. Take a minute to see if you can figure it out. (After 1 minute, give clues if needed.) Add your letters to **subtract** to spell the secret word. <u>He knows all the addition and **subtraction** facts.</u>

**Sort:** Display the words on cards in the order they were made, and have each word read aloud. Have the related words sorted. Talk with students about how the words are related, and have students make sentences that combine the related words.

| art | tour | botanic | traction |
|---|---|---|---|
| artist | tours | botanist | subtract |
| | tourist | | subtraction |

**Transfer:** Have students use the related words to spell and make sentences for similar words:

way/subway   standard/substandard   urban/suburban

### Word Wall Review—Be a Mind Reader (p. 141)
1. It is in the middle section of the alphabet (**I-Q**).
2. It begins with the letter **i**.
3. It begins with the prefix **in**.
4. The prefix **in** means "in."
5. It means **people who come to inspect.**

# Lesson 84

### Letters: a e i o c n r r t t
**Words: enact reactor retract tractor creator creation reaction interact traction retraction**

**Make Words:** Distribute the letters and tell students what words to make. After each word is made, show the correct spelling. Make sure everyone has each word spelled correctly before doing the next word. Keep the lesson fast paced.

1. Take 5 letters and spell **enact**. <u>The council is going to **enact** new drug testing laws.</u>
2. Use 7 letters to spell **reactor**. <u>The submarine was powered by a nuclear **reactor**.</u>
3. Use 7 letters to spell **retract**. <u>When cats play, they **retract** their claws.</u>
4. Use 7 letters to spell **tractor**. <u>My uncle bought a new **tractor**.</u>
5. Use 7 letters to spell **creator**. <u>He was the **creator** of many video games.</u>
6. Use 8 letters to spell **creation**. <u>His newest **creation** is awesome!</u>
7. Add 8 letters to spell **reaction**. <u>The **reaction** to the new game has been phenomenal.</u>
8. Use 8 letters to spell **interact**. <u>It is fun to watch the two puppies **interact**.</u>
9. Use 8 letters to spell **traction**. <u>The new tires gave us excellent **traction**.</u>
10. Now it's time for the secret word. Take a minute to see if you can figure it out. (After 1 minute, give clues if needed.) Add your letters to **traction** to spell the secret word. <u>The information in the article was wrong, and the paper printed a **retraction**.</u>

**Sort:** Display the words on cards in the order they were made, and have each word read aloud. Have the related words sorted. Talk with students about how the words are related and have students make sentences that combine the related words.

| | | |
|---|---|---|
| **enact** | **retract** | **creator** |
| **reactor** | **tractor** | **creation** |
| **reaction** | **traction** | |
| **interact** | **retraction** | |

**Transfer:** Have students use the related words to spell and make sentences for similar words:

**reject/rejection    reflect/reflection    reduce/reduction**

**Word Wall Review—Be a Mind Reader (p. 141)**

1. It is in the middle section of the alphabet (**I-Q**).
2. It begins with the letter **i**.
3. It begins with the prefix **in**.
4. The prefix **in** means "not."
5. **Sign** is the root word.

# Lesson 85 Word Wall

## Word Wall Words: television supervision subtraction retraction tractor

Give everyone a copy of the Take-Home Word Wall (p. 168) and/or place the words on the classroom Word Wall.

## Talk about the Words

All of these words come from the Latin root **vis**, which means "see," or **tract**, which means "drag" or "pull." Something that is **visible** can be seen. Something **attractive** pulls you toward it. Discuss these words and how the prefixes and suffixes affect the meaning.

**television:** The root is **vis** with the prefix **tele** and the suffix **sion**. The prefix **tele** means "far" or "distant." A television allows you to see things that are very far away.

**supervision:** The root is **vis** with the prefix **super** and the suffix **sion**. The prefix **super** means "over" or "beyond." When you **supervise**, you oversee things to make sure they are being done correctly.

**subtraction:** The root is **tract** with the prefix **sub** and the suffix **tion**. The prefix **sub** means "under" or "less than." When you **subtract** something, you pull it away and have less than you started with.

**retraction:** The root is **tract** with the prefix **re** and the suffix **tion**. The prefix **re** means "back" or "again." When you **retract** something, you pull it back.

**tractor:** The root is **tract** with the ~~prefix~~ *suffix* **or**. A **tractor** often pulls a plow.

## Cheer for the Words

Lead the class in cheering for each word in a rhythmic way, emphasizing the morphemic parts of the word "s-u-b—t-r-a-c—t-i-o-n." If possible, cheer for each new word three times.

## Use the Prefixes and Suffixes

Say these sentences aloud, and have students figure out a word with one of the prefixes or suffixes—**sub**, **super**, **re**, **sion**, **tion**—that will make sense in the sentence.

* The things that you **possess** are your _____.
* The ship carrying the **marines** was attacked by an enemy _____.
* The corner **market** was torn down and a huge _____ was built.
* My cut got **infected**, and I had to go to the doctor so he could treat the _____.
* The basketball players **bounded** down the court and scrambled to get the _____.

## Lesson 86

**Letters:** e  o  o  c  j  p  r  r  s  t
**Words:** poor  scoot  troop  troops  poorer  poorest  trooper  scooter  project  projectors

**Make Words:** Distribute the letters and tell students what words to make. After each word is made, show the correct spelling. Make sure everyone has each word spelled correctly before doing the next word. Keep the lesson fast paced.

1.  Take 4 letters and spell **poor**. <u>The people in many countries in Africa are very **poor**.</u>
2.  Use 5 letters to spell **scoot**. <u>**Scoot** down and make room for your brother.</u>
3.  Use 5 letters to spell **troop**. <u>Our Girl Scout **troop** is going camping.</u>
4.  Add a letter and spell **troops**. <u>Girl Scouts from **troops** all over the country will be there.</u>
5.  Use 6 letters to spell **poorer**. <u>We went to visit some of the **poorer** countries in the world.</u>
6.  Use 7 letters to spell **poorest**. <u>Many people in the **poorest** countries earn less than a dollar a day</u>.
7.  Use 7 letters to spell **trooper**. <u>The state **trooper** stopped the speeding car.</u>
8.  Use 7 letters to spell **scooter**. <u>I wish I had a motor **scooter**.</u>
9.  Use 7 letters to spell **project**. <u>He had a booming voice that could **project** across the entire auditorium.</u>
10. Now it's time for the secret word. Take a minute to see if you can figure it out. (After 1 minute, give clues if needed.) Add your letters to **project** to spell the secret word. <u>The town set up a big screen and **projectors** in the stadium so we could all watch the soccer game.</u>

**Sort:** Display the words on cards in the order they were made, and have each word read aloud. Have the related words sorted. Talk with students about how the words are related, and have students make sentences that combine the related words.

| | | | |
|---|---|---|---|
| scoot | troop | poor | project |
| scooter | troops | poorer | projectors |
| | trooper | poorest | |

**Transfer:** Have students use the related words to spell and make sentences for similar words:

rich/richer/richest  great/greater/greatest  inspect/inspectors  connect/connectors

**Word Wall Review—Be a Mind Reader (p. 141)**

1.  It is in the last section of the alphabet (**S-Z**).
2.  It includes the letter **r**.
3.  It does not include the letter n.
4.  It has 7 letters.
5.  **Tract** is the root.

# Lesson 87

### Letters: e i o o b c j n s t
### Words: nice join note notes joints nicest notice inject object objections

**Make Words:** Distribute the letters and tell students what words to make. After each word is made, show the correct spelling. Make sure everyone has each word spelled correctly before doing the next word. Keep the lesson fast paced.

1. Take 4 letters and spell **nice**. Your aunt is a very **nice** person.
2. Use 4 letters to spell **join**. We will **join** the club.
3. Use 4 letters to spell **note**. I will send her a **note**.
4. Add a letter to spell **notes**. We took **notes** during our field trip.
5. Use 6 letters to spell **joints**. Your elbows, knees, and wrists have **joints** where two bones come together.
6. Use 6 letters to spell **nicest**. Yesterday was the **nicest** day.
7. Use 6 letters to spell **notice**. I will send everyone a **notice** about our next meeting.
8. Use 6 letters to spell **inject**. My dad will always **inject** some humorous comment into our conversations.
9. Change 2 letters and spell **object**. I hope my dad will not **object** to my plans for the trip.
10. Now it's time for the secret word. Take a minute to see if you can figure it out. (After 1 minute, give clues if needed.) Add your letters to **object** to spell the secret word. Fortunately, my dad had no **objections** to my plans.

**Sort:** Display the words on cards in the order they were made, and have each word read aloud. Have the related words sorted. Talk with students about how the words are related, and have students make sentences that combine the related words.

| join | nice | note | inject |
|------|------|------|--------|
| joints | nicest | notes | object |
| | | notice | objections |

**Transfer:** Have students use the related words to spell and make sentences for similar words:

**happy/happiest   funny/funniest   busy/busiest   injections**

## Word Wall Review—Be a Mind Reader (p. 141)

1. It is in the last section of the alphabet (**S-Z**).
2. It begins with the letter **t**.
3. Act is not the root.
4. **Trans** is the prefix.
5. It includes planes, ships, cars, trucks, buses, and subways.

# Lesson 88

**Letters:** e  i  i  u  d  n  n  p  r  s
**Words:** sun  pin  ripe  ripen  unpin  unripe  sunnier  inspire  inspired  uninspired

**Make Words:** Distribute the letters and tell students what words to make. After each word is made, show the correct spelling. Make sure everyone has each word spelled correctly before doing the next word. Keep the lesson fast paced.

1. Take 3 letters and spell **sun**. After three days of rain, we were delighted to see the **sun**.
2. Use 3 letters to spell **pin**. She wore a pretty **pin**.
3. Use 4 letters to spell **ripe**. The bananas are almost **ripe**.
4. Add a letter to spell **ripen**. They should **ripen** in a few days.
5. Add 2 letters to spell **unpin**. Can you help me **unpin** this?
6. Use 6 letters to spell **unripe**. It is not good to eat **unripe** bananas.
7. Use 7 letters to spell **sunnier**. Today was **sunnier** than yesterday.
8. Use 7 letters to spell **inspire**. The coach hoped his speech would **inspire** the team to go the extra mile.
9. Add a letter to spell **inspired**. They came on to the field **inspired**.
10. Now it's time for the secret word. Take a minute to see if you can figure it out. (After 1 minute, give clues if needed.) Add your letters to **inspired** to spell the secret word. The opposite of inspired is **uninspired**.

**Sort:** Display the words on cards in the order they were made, and have each word read aloud. Have the related words sorted. Talk with students about how the words are related, and have students make sentences that combine the related words.

| sun | pin | ripe | inspire |
|---|---|---|---|
| sunnier | unpin | ripen | inspired |
| | | unripe | uninspired |

**Transfer:** Have students use the related words to spell and make sentences for similar words:

broke/broken/unbroken  beat/beaten/unbeaten  write/written/unwritten

**Word Wall Review—Be a Mind Reader (p. 141)**

1. It is in the last section of the alphabet (**R-Z**).
2. It begins with the letter **s**.
3. It does not have a prefix.
4. **Sign** is the root.
5. It is **what you have when you sign your name**.

# Lesson 89

## Letters: a  i  o  o  c  n  p  r  r  s  s  t
**Words:** port  arson  cross  across  airport  arsonist  scorpion  scorpions  conspirator  conspirators

**Make Words:** Distribute the letters and tell students what words to make. After each word is made, show the correct spelling. Make sure everyone has each word spelled correctly before doing the next word. Keep the lesson fast paced.

1. Take 5 letters and spell **port**. The ship came into **port**.
2. Use 5 letters to spell **arson**. **Arson** was the cause of the fire.
3. Use 5 letters to spell **cross**. Look both ways before you **cross** the street.
4. Add a letter to spell **across**. His house is **across** the street from mine.
5. Use 7 letters to spell **airport**. Planes land every minute at the busy **airport**.
6. Use 8 letters to spell **arsonist**. The police arrested the **arsonist** who started the fire.
7. Use 8 letters to spell **scorpion**. She got bitten by a **scorpion**.
8. Add a letter to spell **scorpions**. Some **scorpions** are 8 inches long.
9. Use 11 letters to spell **conspirator**. He was indicted as a **conspirator** in the kidnapping.
10. Now it's time for the secret word. Take a minute to see if you can figure it out. (After 1 minute, give clues if needed.) Add your letters to **conspirator** to spell the secret word. The **conspirators** met and planned the kidnapping.

**Sort:** Display the words on cards in the order they were made, and have each word read aloud. Have the related words sorted. Talk with students about how the words are related, and have students make sentences that combine the related words.

| port | cross | arson | scorpion | conspirator |
| airport | across | arsonist | scorpions | conspirators |

**Transfer:** Have students use the related words to spell and make sentences for similar words:

plane/airplane  bag/airbag  strip/airstrip  long/along  round/around

## Word Wall Review—Be a Mind Reader (p. 141)

1. It is in the last section of the alphabet (**R-Z**).
2. It begins with the letter **s**.
3. Sign is not the root.
4. It has a prefix.
5. **Tract** is the root.

# Lesson 90 Word Wall

**Word Wall Words: projectors objections inject uninspired conspirators**

Give everyone a copy of the Take-Home Word Wall (p. 169) and/or place the words on the classroom Word Wall.

## Talk about the Words:

All of these words come from the Latin root **jec**, which means, "throw," or **spir**, which means "breathe." When you **eject** someone, you throw them out. When you **reject** something, you throw it back. Your **respiratory** system includes the organs in your body that let you breathe.

**projectors:** The root is **jec** with the prefix **pro**, the suffix **or**, and the **s** ending. The prefix **pro** sometimes means "forward." When you **project**, you throw something forward. Movie **projectors** "throw" the image forward onto the screen.

**objections:** The root is **jec** with the prefix **ob**, the suffix **tion**, and the **s** ending. The prefix **ob** sometimes means "against." When you **object**, you throw something against the plan. **Objections** are arguments against something. During a trial, attorneys **object** if they think some testimony or questions are unfair. The judge says, "**objection** sustained" or "**objection** overruled."

**inject:** The root is **jec** with the prefix **in**. When you **inject** something, you throw it in.

**uninspired:** The root is **spir** with the prefixes **un** and **in** and the ending **ed**. **Uninspired** is the opposite of **inspired**.

**conspirators:** The root is **spir** with the prefix **con**, the suffix **or**, and the **s** ending. The prefix **con** often means "with" or "together." When you **conspire** with others, you "breathe together" quietly and in secret. **Conspirators** are people who **conspire**.

## Cheer for the Words

Lead the class in cheering for each word in a rhythmic way, emphasizing the morphemic parts of the word "**o-b—j-e-c—t-i-o-n-s**." If possible, cheer for each new word three times.

## Use the Prefixes and Suffixes

Say these sentences aloud, and have students figure out a word with one of the prefixes or suffixes—**pro**, **un**, **con**, **or**, **tion**—that will make sense in the sentence.

- When you drive or force something back, you **repel** it. When you drive or force something forward, you _____ it.
- Tearing something down is **destruction**. Building something is _____.
- I had planned to **finish** painting the house that day, but when I fell off the ladder, I had to leave the job _____ for several weeks.
- People who **direct** movies are called _____.
- When you **direct** someone, you give them_____.

106        CD-2420 Big Words for Big Kids        © Carson-Dellosa

# Lesson 91

### Letters: e i i o u c f n s t
### Words: fit fits note notes unfit notice infect infects notifies infectious

**Make Words:** Distribute the letters and tell students what words to make. After each word is made, show the correct spelling. Make sure everyone has each word spelled correctly before doing the next word. Keep the lesson fast paced.

1. Take 3 letters and spell **fit**. <u>She worked out every day and was very **fit**</u>.
2. Add a letter to spell **fits**. <u>Try this shoe on and see how it **fits**</u>.
3. Use 4 letters to spell **note**. <u>I made a **note** of the time of our appointment</u>.
4. Add a letter and spell **notes**. <u>The secretary took **notes** at the meeting</u>.
5. Use 5 letters to spell **unfit**. <u>The trial was postponed because the defendant was **unfit** to stand trial</u>.
6. Use 6 letters to spell **notice**. <u>I did not **notice** what kind of car they were driving</u>.
7. Use 6 letters to spell **infect**. <u>A virus can **infect** your computer's hard drive</u>.
8. Add a letter to spell **infects**. <u>The strep virus **infects** a lot of people each year</u>.
9. Use 8 letters to spell **notifies**. <u>The president **notifies** everyone of any changes in the schedule</u>.
10. Now it's time for the secret word. Take a minute to see if you can figure it out. (After 1 minute, give clues if needed.) Add your letters to a word you have already made to spell the secret word. <u>Measles is an **infectious** disease</u>.

**Sort:** Display the words on cards in the order they were made, and have each word read aloud. Have the related words sorted. Talk with students about how the words are related, and have students make sentences that combine the related words.

| fit | note | infect |
|-----|------|--------|
| fits | notes | infects |
| unfit | notice | infectious |
| | notifies | |

**Transfer:** Have students use the related words to spell and make sentences for similar words:

caution/cautious  nutrition/nutritious  ambition/ambitious

### Word Wall Review—Be a Mind Reader (p. 141)

1. It is in the middle section of the alphabet (**I-Q**).
2. It begins with the letter **p**.
3. Power is not the root.
4. **Pre** is the prefix.
5. It means **you know things will happen before they happen**.

# Lesson 92

### Letters: e  e  i  c  f  l  m  p  r  t  y
### Words: firm  creep  creepy  firmly  fierce  fiercely  perfect  imperfect  perfectly  imperfectly

**Make Words:** Distribute the letters and tell students what words to make. After each word is made, show the correct spelling. Make sure everyone has each word spelled correctly before doing the next word. Keep the lesson fast paced.

1. Take 4 letters and spell **firm**. The foundation was **firm** and strong.
2. Use 5 letters to spell **creep**. The cat began to **creep** toward the mouse.
3. Add a letter to spell **creepy**. I don't like **creepy**, crawly creatures.
4. Use 6 letters to spell **firmly**. Pat the soil down **firmly** around the plant.
5. Use 6 letters to spell **fierce**. The lion looked very **fierce**.
6. Add 2 letters to spell **fiercely**. He growled **fiercely**.
7. Use 7 letters to spell **perfect**. Today was a **perfect** day.
8. Add 2 letters to spell **imperfect**. **Imperfect** is the opposite of perfect.
9. Use 9 letters to spell **perfectly**. She was **perfectly** happy to sit on the beach and watch the waves roll in.
10. Now it's time for the secret word. Take a minute to see if you can figure it out. (After 1 minute, give clues if needed.) Add your letters to **perfectly** to spell the secret word. The opposite of perfectly is **imperfectly**.

**Sort:** Display the words on cards in the order they were made, and have each word read aloud. Have the related words sorted. Talk with students about how the words are related, and have students make sentences that combine the related words.

| firm | creep | fierce | perfect |
|------|-------|--------|---------|
| firmly | creepy | fiercely | perfectly |
|  |  |  | imperfect |
|  |  |  | imperfectly |

**Transfer:** Have students use the related words to spell and make sentences for similar words:

**sleep/sleepy  polite/politely/impolitely  patient/impatient/impatiently**

### Word Wall Review—Be a Mind Reader (p. 141)

1. It is in the middle section of the alphabet (**I-Q**).
2. It begins with the letter **p**.
3. Power is not the root.
4. Pre is not the prefix.
5. **Pro** is the prefix.

# Lesson 93

## Letters: i o o u c c n n r s t t
## Words: tour riot riots tours tourist riotous unicorn unicorns construct construction

**Make Words:** Distribute the letters and tell students what words to make. After each word is made, show the correct spelling. Make sure everyone has each word spelled correctly before doing the next word. Keep the lesson fast paced.

1. Take 4 letters and spell **tour**. <u>We took a **tour** of the White House.</u>
2. Take 4 letters and spell **riot**. <u>The **riot** started when someone threw a bottle.</u>
3. Add a letter to spell **riots**. <u>The police quickly ended the **riots**.</u>
4. Use 5 letters to spell **tours**. <u>The retired people took many bus **tours**.</u>
5. Use 7 letters to spell **tourist**. <u>We got brochures at the **tourist** information center.</u>
6. Use 7 letters to spell **riotous**. <u>The crowd turned into a **riotous** mob.</u>
7. Use 7 letters to spell **unicorn**. <u>A **unicorn** has one horn on top of its head.</u>
8. Add a letter to spell **unicorns**. <u>**Unicorns** are imaginary creatures.</u>
9. Use 9 letters to spell **construct**. <u>They are going to **construct** a new building on the site of the old one.</u>
10. Now it's time for the secret word. Take a minute to see if you can figure it out. (After 1 minute, give clues if needed.) Add your letters to **construct** to spell the secret word. <u>The **construction** crews have already begun working.</u>

**Sort:** Display the words on cards in the order they were made, and have each word read aloud. Have the related words sorted. Talk with students about how the words are related, and have students make sentences that combine the related words.

| | | | |
|---|---|---|---|
| riot | tour | unicorn | construct |
| riots | tours | unicorns | construction |
| riotous | tourist | | |

**Transfer:** Have students use the related words to spell and make sentences for similar words:

**instruct/instruction   destruct/destruction   reconstruct/reconstruction**

## Word Wall Review—Be a Mind Reader (p. 141)

1. It is in the first section of the alphabet (**A-H**).
2. It has a prefix and a suffix.
3. It does not begin with the letter d.
4. It does not begin with the letter e.
5. It begins with the prefix **contra**.

# Lesson 94

## Letters: e e i i u b c d l n r s t t
### Words: trust  unite  listed  secure  entrust  reunite  destruct  unlisted  insecure  destructible  indestructible

**Make Words:** Distribute the letters and tell students what words to make. After each word is made, show the correct spelling. Make sure everyone has each word spelled correctly before doing the next word. Keep the lesson fast paced.

1. Take 5 letters and spell **trust**. He chose someone he could **trust** for the important mission.
2. Use 5 letters to spell **unite**. All the people had to **unite** to fight the war.
3. Use 6 letters to spell **listed**. Is your phone number **listed** in the book?
4. Use 6 letters to spell **secure**. We live in a safe, **secure** neighborhood.
5. Use 7 letters to spell **entrust**. While I am away, I **entrust** him with the care of my house.
6. Use 7 letters to spell **reunite**. They are making every effort to **reunite** the refugees with their families.
7. Use 7 letters to spell **destruct**. The scientist was forced to **destruct** the missile shortly after its launch.
8. Use 8 letters to spell **unlisted**. Her phone number is **unlisted**.
9. Use 8 letters to spell **insecure**. The opposite of secure is **insecure**.
10. Use 12 letters to spell **destructible**. The enemy attacked all **destructible** targets.
11. Now it's time for the secret word. Take a minute to see if you can figure it out. (After 1 minute, give clues if needed.) Add your letters to **destructible** to spell the secret word. Very few things are **indestructible**.

**Sort:** Display the words on cards in the order they were made, and have each word read aloud. Have the related words sorted. Talk with students about how the words are related, and have students make sentences that combine the related words.

| trust | listed | secure | unite | destruct |
|---|---|---|---|---|
| entrust | unlisted | insecure | reunite | destructible |
| | | | | indestructible |

**Transfer:** Have students use the related words to spell and make sentences for similar words:

edible/inedible  credible/incredible  respond/responsible/irresponsible

**Word Wall Review—Be a Mind Reader (p. 141)**

1. It is in the first section of the alphabet (**A-H**).
2. It has a prefix and a suffix.
3. It does not begin with the letter d.
4. It does not begin with the letter e.
5. It means **people who conspire together**.

Give everyone a copy of the Take-Home Word Wall (p. 170) and/or place the words on the classroom Word Wall.

## Talk about the Words

All of these words come from the Latin root **fec**, which means "make" or "do," or **struct**, which means "build." When you **effect** something, you make it happen. A **structure** is something you build.

**infectious:** The root is **fec** with the prefix **in** and the suffix **ous**. The prefix **in** sometimes means "in." An **infection** does something in your body. **Infectious** describes an **infection**.

**perfectly:** The root is **fec** with the prefix **per** and the suffix **ly**. The prefix **per** sometimes means "through." Something that is done **perfectly** is done well all of the way through.

**imperfectly:** The root is **fec** with the prefixes **im** and **per** and the suffix **ly**. The prefix **im** sometimes means "opposite" or "not." **Imperfectly** is the opposite of **perfectly**.

**construction:** The root is **struct** with the prefix **con** and the suffix **tion**. The prefix **con** sometimes means "together." **Construction** is something you build together.

**indestructible:** The root is **struct** with the prefixes **in** and **de** and the suffix **ible**. The prefix **de** sometimes means "opposite." **Destruct** is the opposite of **construct**. Something that is **destructible** can be **destroyed**. **Indestructible** is the opposite of **destructible**.

## Cheer for the Words

Lead the class in cheering for each word in a rhythmic way, emphasizing the morphemic parts of the word "i-m—p-e-r—f-e-c-t—l-y." If possible, cheer for each new word three times.

## Use the Prefixes and Suffixes

Say these sentences aloud, and have students figure out a word with one of the prefixes or suffixes—**im**, **in**, **ly**, **ible**, **tion**—that will make sense in the sentence.

- A person with common **sense** makes _____ decisions.
- The opposite of **visible** is _____.
- The opposite of **patient** is _____.
- Because of the drought, the city had to **restrict** water use. Many citizens did not like these _____.
- When you do something in a **careful** way, you do it _____.

# Lesson 96

### Letters: i i o o b g l s s t
### Words: lost loss solo tool toil toils tools soloist biologist biologists

**Make Words:** Distribute the letters and tell students what words to make. After each word is made, show the correct spelling. Make sure everyone has each word spelled correctly before doing the next word. Keep the lesson fast paced.

1. Take 4 letters and spell **lost**. Have you ever gotten **lost**?
2. Change a letter to spell **loss**. His early death was a great **loss** to his family and his country.
3. Use 4 letters to spell **solo**. He is making his first **solo** flight.
4. Use 4 letters and spell **tool**. Where is my **tool** kit?
5. Change 1 letter to spell **toil**. The workers **toil** long hours picking the crops.
6. Add a letter to spell **toils**. She told her grandchildren about all her **toils** and troubles.
7. Change 1 letter to spell **tools**. All of my **tools** are in my tool kit.
8. Use 7 letters to spell **soloist**. She was the lead **soloist** in the choir.
9. Use 9 letters to spell **biologist**. When I grow up, I want to be a **biologist**.
10. Now it's time for the secret word. Take a minute to see if you can figure it out. (After 1 minute, give clues if needed.) Add your letters to **biologist** to spell the secret word. **Biologists** do research on all forms of life.

**Sort:** Display the words on cards in the order they were made, and have each word read aloud. Have the related words sorted. Talk with students about how the words are related, and have students make sentences that combine the related words.

| | | | | |
|---|---|---|---|---|
| lost | tool | toil | solo | biologist |
| loss | tools | toils | soloist | biologists |

**Transfer:** Have students use the related words to spell and make sentences for similar words:

science/scientist   physics/physicist   pharmacy/pharmacist

**Word Wall Review—Be a Mind Reader (p. 141)**

1. It is in the middle section of the alphabet (**I-Q**).
2. It begins with the letter **i**.
3. **Inter** is the prefix.
4. Act is not the root.
5. It means **something between nations**.

**Make Words:** Distribute the letters and tell students what words to make. After each word is made, show the correct spelling. Make sure everyone has each word spelled correctly before doing the next word. Keep the lesson fast paced.

1. Take 4 letters and spell **taco**. <u>I ordered a **taco** and an enchilada.</u>
2. Add a letter to spell **tacos**. <u>I like tomatoes on my **tacos**.</u>
3. Use 6 letters to spell **titans**. <u>In Greek myths, **titans** were giants who ruled the world.</u>
4. Use 6 letters to spell **bionic**. <u>Did you ever see the movies about the **bionic** man and the **bionic** woman</u>?
5. Use 6 letters to spell **action.** <u>My brother likes movies with lots of **action**.</u>
6. Add a letter to spell **actions**. <u>She shocked everyone with her rude words and **actions**.</u>
7. Use 7 letters to spell **titanic**. <u>The **_Titanic_** was a giant ship.</u>
8. Use 7 letters to spell **botanic**. <u>Our science class visited the **botanic** gardens.</u>
9. Use 8 letters to spell **botanist**. <u>Our tour guide was studying to be a **botanist**.</u>
10. Now it's time for the secret word. Take a minute to see if you can figure it out. (After 1 minute, give clues if needed.) The secret word begins with the prefix **anti**. <u>I took **antibiotics** for two weeks to fight my infection.</u>

**Sort:** Display the words on cards in the order they were made, and have each word read aloud. Have the related words sorted. Talk with students about how the words are related, and have students make sentences that combine the related words.

| taco | titans | action | botanic | bionic |
|------|--------|--------|---------|--------|
| tacos | Titanic | actions | botanist | antibiotics |

**Transfer:** Have students use the related words to spell and make sentences for similar words:

war/antiwar   bodies/antibodies   social/antisocial

**Word Wall Review—Be a Mind Reader (p. 141)**

1. It is in the middle section of the alphabet (**I-Q**).
2. It begins with the letter **i**.
3. It has 10 letters.
4. **In** is the prefix.
5. It ends in **ous**.

# Lesson 98

### Letters: e e i i b c d l n r
### Words: bled bred breed bleed blend edible blender inedible credible incredible

**Make Words:** Distribute the letters and tell students what words to make. After each word is made, show the correct spelling. Make sure everyone has each word spelled correctly before doing the next word. Keep the lesson fast paced.

1.  Take 4 letters and spell **bled**. <u>His cut leg **bled** all over the floor.</u>
2.  Change a letter and spell **bred**. <u>The horses were **bred** to race.</u>
3.  Add a letter to spell **breed**. <u>What **breed** is your dog?</u>
4.  Change a letter to spell **bleed**. <u>Sometimes my gums **bleed** when I brush my teeth.</u>
5.  Change a letter to spell **blend**. <u>**Blend** all of the ingredients together.</u>
6.  Use 6 letters to spell **edible**. <u>Some mushrooms are **edible**.</u>
7.  Use 7 letters to spell **blender**. <u>You can blend things in a **blender**.</u>
8.  Use 8 letters to spell **inedible**. <u>Some mushrooms are **inedible**.</u>
9.  Change 2 letters to spell **credible**. <u>They have to have **credible** evidence before they can charge you with a crime.</u>
10. Now it's time for the secret word. Take a minute to see if you can figure it out. (After 1 minute, give clues if needed.) Add your letters to **credible** to spell the secret word. <u>That's **incredible**!</u>

**Sort:** Display the words on cards in the order they were made, and have each word read aloud. Have the related words sorted. Talk with students about how the words are related, and have students make sentences that combine the related words.

| bred | bled | blend | edible | credible |
|---|---|---|---|---|
| breed | bleed | blender | inedible | incredible |

**Transfer:** Have students use the related words to spell and make sentences for similar words:

visible/invisible  flexible/inflexible  possible/impossible

## Word Wall Review—Be a Mind Reader (p. 141)

1.  It is in the middle section of the alphabet (**I-Q**).
2.  It begins with the letter **i**.
3.  It begins with the prefix **in**.
4.  **Depend** is the root.
5.  It ends in **ence**.

# Lesson 99

### Letters: e  i  o  c  d  r  r  s  t
### Words: edit  riot  ride  riders  rioters  editors  credits  directs  directors  creditors

**Make Words:** Distribute the letters and tell students what words to make. After each word is made, show the correct spelling. Make sure everyone has each word spelled correctly before doing the next word. Keep the lesson fast paced.

1. Take 4 letters and spell **edit**. His job is to **edit** the newspaper articles.
2. Use 4 letters to spell **riot**. The **riot** started when the home team lost.
3. Use 4 letters to spell **ride**. We went for a **ride** on his new motorcycle.
4. Add 2 letters to spell **riders**. Motorcycle **riders** need to wear helmets.
5. Use 7 letters to spell **rioters**. The police arrested the **rioters**.
6. Use 7 letters to spell **editors**. The **editors** of all of the sections of the paper held a meeting.
7. Use 7 letters to spell **credits**. I like to read the **credits** at the end of a movie.
8. Move the letters to spell **directs**. My cousin **directs** movies.
9. Today there are 2 secret words. (Let students try to figure them out.) The **directors** of the movies needed to borrow money. The people who loaned them the money are called **creditors**.

**Sort:** Display the words on cards in the order they were made, and have each word read aloud. Have the related words sorted. Talk with students about how the words are related, and have students make sentences that combine the related words.

| ride | riot | edit | directs | credits |
|------|------|------|---------|---------|
| riders | rioters | editors | directors | creditors |

**Transfer:** Have students use the related words to spell and make sentences for similar words:

edible/inedible  credible/incredible  respond/responsible/irresponsible

## Word Wall Review—Be a Mind Reader (p. 141)

1. It is in the middle section of the alphabet (**I-Q**).
2. It begins with the letter **i**.
3. It does not begin with the prefix im.
4. It does not begin with the prefix inter.
5. It means **the opposite of destructible**.

# Lesson 100  Word Wall

**Word Wall Words: biologists  bionic  antibiotics  incredible  creditors**

Give everyone a copy of the Take-Home Word Wall (p. 171) and/or place the words on the classroom Word Wall.

## Talk about the Words

All of these words come from the Latin root **bio**, which means "life," or **cred**, which means "believe" or "trust." **Biology** is the study of living things. Something that is **credible** is believable.

**biologists:** The root is **bio** with the suffix **is**, and the **s** ending. The suffix **ist** sometimes means "person." **Biologists** work in **biology**. Scientists do science. Pianists play the piano. Guitarists play the guitar.

**bionic:** The root is **bio** with the suffix **ic**. **Bionic** means a living thing, often with artificial parts. It is a popular concept in science fiction.

**antibiotics:** The root is **bio** with the prefix **anti**, the suffix **ic**, and the **s** ending. The prefix **anti** sometimes means "against." **Antibiotics** work against bacteria and other microorganisms. **Antihistamines**, such as Benadryl®, work against the histamines that cause sneezing and itching.

**incredible:** The root is **cred** with the prefix **in** and the suffix **ible**. Something that is **credible** is believable. Something that is **incredible** is unbelievable.

**creditors:** The root is **cred** with the suffix **or** and the **s** ending. **Creditors** give you credit or loan you money because they believe or trust that you will pay what you owe.

## Cheer for the Words

Lead the class in cheering for each word in a rhythmic way, emphasizing the morphemic parts of the word "i-n—c-r-e-d—i-b-l-e." If possible, cheer for each new word three times.

## Use the Prefixes and Suffixes

Say these sentences aloud, and have students figure out a word with one of the prefixes or suffixes—**in, anti, or, ist, ic**—that will make sense in the sentence.

- I don't want my car engine to **freeze**, so I am going to make sure it has plenty of _____.
- The opposite of **expensive** is _____.
- A person who writes a newspaper **column** is called a _____.
- The person who **conducts** the orchestra is the _____.
- People who have a lot of **energy** are _____.

*CD-2420 Big Words for Big Kids*

# Review Activities

These review activities can be done when all of the lessons are completed or whenever you feel the need and have the time to review important concepts. The examples include all 100 Word Wall words and all of the words used in the Making Words lessons. If you use these activities before you have finished the lessons, adjust the list to include only those words used so far. Save the word cards you make for each lesson, and file them alphabetically so you can find them quickly. (CD-2812 Big Words for Big Kids Word Card Set is also available and contains all of the word cards needed for all of the lessons.) Display the words you want to work on. Review by calling out the words and having students chant and write them or by giving sentence clues to words and having students decide which word fits in the sentence. You can also review the words by playing WORDO (p. 143) or Be a Mind Reader (p. 141).

## Words Organized by Prefix or Suffix

| Prefix | Word Wall Word | Other Words Made |
|---|---|---|
| **a/ad (to, toward)** | assignment | across aside asleep assign agree agreement admit readmit |
| **anti (against)** | antibiotics | antisocial |
| **com/con (with, together)** | composers | compose compress |
| | conspirators | conspirator conspire conspires conspired |
| | construction | construct contract contraction |
| **contra (against)** | contradictions | contradict |
| **de (opposite, down)** | demagnetize | deport design redesign designer |
| | declassify | depend dependent dependence |
| | deformity | deform detain detainee |
| | depressing | depress |
| | indestructible | destruct destructible |
| **dis (not, do the opposite)** | displeased | disgrace disease diseased |
| | discovery | discover |
| | disappearance | disappear |
| | discouraged | distract distraction |
| **en (make)** | encouragement | enact encourage enforce enlist |
| | encouraging | ensure entrap entrust |

| | | |
|---|---|---|
| **e/ex (out)** | expression | express expose |
| | exportable | export |
| | emission | event |
| **im/in (in)** | unimpressive | impress impression impressive |
| | importance | import |
| | inspectors | inspect inspector |
| | inventor | invent invention indent indented |
| | uninspired | intend intended inspire inspired |
| | inject | inmate |
| | infectious | infect infects |
| | | |
| **im/in/ir (not)** | impossibility | impossible |
| | imperfectly | imperfect impure |
| | independence | inactive |
| | independent | intolerant |
| | insignificant | insecure insane |
| | incredible | inedible indirect |
| | indestructible | |
| | irreplaceable | |
| | | |
| **inter (between, among)** | interactive | interact Internet |
| | international | |
| | intervention | |
| | | |
| **mis (wrong, badly)** | misplaced | misdeal misdealing |
| | misleading | mislead mistreat |
| | | |
| **ob** | objections | object |
| | | |
| **per (through)** | performance | perform |
| | permission | |
| | imperfectly | imperfect |
| | perfectly | perfect |
| | | |
| **pre (before, earlier)** | predictions | predict |
| | unpredictable | predictable prepare prepared |
| | prevention | prevent prepaid preset |
| | | |
| **pro (for, forward)** | projectors | promise promises |

CD-2420 Big Words for Big Kids

| re (back, again) | reactions | react reaction reactor |
| | resignation | resign readmit rebuild recover |
| | recreation | redesign redo reset |
| | irreplaceable | replace reread resale reseal reseat |
| | reappeared | remit reopen recall |
| | reformed | reform regain reheat |
| | reporters | report reunite retrace |
| | repress | reuse reusing |
| | retraction | retract review |
| **sub (under, less)** | subtraction | subtract |
| **super (beyond, more)** | supervision | |
| **tele (far)** | television | |
| **trans (across)** | transaction | transact |
| | transportation | transport |
| | transmitted | transmit |
| **un (not, opposite)** | unhealthiest | untie untied |
| | unimpressive | unripe unpin unlisted |
| | unpredictable | unfit uneaten |
| | uninspired | uncaring unaltered |
| | uncovered | |
| **under (under, beneath)** | underweight | |
| | undercover | |
| **over (over, beyond)** | overweight | overrun overdue |

| Suffix | Word Wall Word | Other Words Made |
|---|---|---|
| en | brighten | deepen deepened eaten liven proven |
| | ripen | risen rotten stolen uneaten |
| er/est | brightest | lower nicer nicest cooler cuter deeper |
| | healthier | nosier later slower sunnier tighter |
| | unhealthiest | healthiest poorer poorest riper |
| | fuller | iciest neatest rainiest angriest |

| | | |
|---|---|---|
| **ify (y changes to i)** | declassify<br>classification | classify notifies |
| **ize** | demagnetize<br>pressurized | magnetize |
| **ate** | formulates | hesitate operate create |
| **less** | powerless | |
| **ful** | powerful<br>powerfully | tearful armful |
| **able/ible** | operable<br>irreplaceable<br>exportable<br>portable<br>unpredictable<br>indestructible<br>incredible<br>impossibility | predictable<br><br><br><br><br>edible inedible destructible<br>credible |
| **sion/tion** | recreation<br>transportation<br><br>classification<br>resignation<br>reactions<br>transaction<br>predictions<br>contradictions<br>intervention<br>retraction<br>subtraction<br>prevention<br>construction<br>expression<br>emission<br>permission<br>television<br>supervision | action actions alienation alteration<br>carnation carnations contraction<br>creation<br>donation fiction fictional<br>reaction traction invention nation<br>national nationalities nations<br><br><br><br><br><br><br><br><br>impression mission<br><br><br>vision |

CD-2420 Big Words for Big Kids

| **ly** | powerfully | fiercely firmly fully impossibly |
| | courageously | lowly perfectly possibly safely |
| | imperfectly | |
| | perfectly | |

| **er/or** | reporters | healer heater leader loser opener poster |
| | composers | racer reader riders rioters scooter sealer |
| | leadership | signer singer singers sitter stingers |
| | dealership | timer toaster trainer trooper voter |
| | blender | caller camper caterer coaster |
| | cooler | copier dancer dealer designer |
| | dieter | diver eaters farmer |
| | actors | reactor spectator visors conspirator |
| | creator | dictators directors donors editor |
| | dictatorship | editors inspector inventor |
| | dictator | |
| | spectators | |
| | inventor | |
| | inspectors | |
| | tractor | |
| | conspirators | |
| | projectors | |
| | creditors | |

| **ist** | biologists | arsonist artist biologist botanist cartoonist |
| | finalists | novelist organist racist socialist |
| | soloist | tourist |

| **ess** | actresses | princess |

| **ance/ence** | disappearance | |
| | performance | |
| | importance | |
| | independence | dependence |

| **ment** | encouragement | agreement argument |
| | assignment | |

| | | |
|---|---|---|
| **ness** | brightness | |
| **y/ity (y changes to i)** | discovery | |
| | deformity | |
| | impossibility | |
| | nationalities | |
| **sure/ture** | pleasures | |
| | pressurized | pressure  pressured |
| | creatures | |
| | signature | |
| **ant/ent** | significant | |
| | insignificant | |
| | independent | dependent |
| **al** | international | |
| | national | |
| | nationalities | |
| | formal | |
| **ive** | interactive | active  inactive  creative |
| | unimpressive | impressive |
| **ous** | courageous | gracious  riotous |
| | courageously | |
| | infectious | |
| **ic** | magnetic | artistic  botanic  medic  patriotic |
| | classic | romantic  Titanic |
| | bionic | |
| | antibiotics | |
| **ship** | leadership | |
| | dealership | |
| | dictatorship | |

CD-2420 Big Words for Big Kids

## Words Organized by Root  (Word Wall Roots)

**act**
act
acting
action
actions
active
actor
actors
actress
actresses
distract
distraction
enact
inactive
interact
interactive
react
reaction
reactions
reactor
transact
transaction

**appear**
appear
appeared
disappear
disappearance
reappeared

**bio**
antibiotics
biologist
biologists
bionic

**bright**
bright
brighten
brightest
brightness

**class**
class
classic
classification
classify
classy
declassify

**courage**
courage
courageous
courageously
discouraged
encourage
encouragement
encouraging

**cover**
cover
covered
discover
discovery
recover
uncovered
undercover

**create**
create
creates
creation
creative
creator
creatures
recreation

**cred**
credible
creditors
credits
incredible

**deal**
deal
dealer
dealership
misdeal
misdealing

**depend**
depend
dependence
dependent
independence
independent

**dic**
contradict
contradictions
dictator
dictators
dictatorship
predict
predictable
predictions
unpredictable

**fec**
imperfect
imperfectly
infect
infectious
infects
perfect
perfectly

**form**
deform
deformity
format
formed
formula
formulates
perform
performance
reform
reformed

**health**
heal
healer
health
healthier
healthiest
unhealthiest

**jec**
inject
object
objections
project
projectors

**lead**
lead
leader
leadership
mislead
misleading

**magnet**
demagnetize
magnet
magnetic
magnetize
magnets

**mis/mit**
admit
emission
mission
omit
omits
permission
promise
promises
readmit
remit

**nation**
international
nation
national
nationalities
nations

**place**
irreplaceable
misplaced
place
placed
places
replace

**please**
displeased
please

pleasures

**port**
airport
deport
export
exportable
import
importance
port
portable
report
reporters
transport
transportation

**pos**
compose
composers
expose
impossibility
impossibly
possibility
possibly
pose
post
poster

**power**
power
powerful
powerfully
powerless

**press**
compress
depress
depressing
express
expression
impress
impression
impressive
press
pressed
pressing
pressure
pressured
pressurized

repress
unimpressive

**sign**
assign
assignment
design
designer
insignificant
redesign
resign
resignation
sign
signal
signaled
signature
signed
signer
significant
signs

**spec**
inspect
inspector
inspectors
spectator
spectators

**spir**
conspirator
conspirators
conspire
conspired
conspires
inspire
inspired
inspires
uninspired

**struct**
construct
construction
destruct

agree
agreement

alien
alienation

alter
alteration
altered
unaltered

anger
angriest

argue
argument

arm
armful
arms

arson
arsonist

art
artist
artistic

be
being

bit
bite

bled
bleed

blend
blender

boss
bossy

botanic
botanist

bred
breed

build
rebuild

call
caller
recall

camp
camper

canoe
canoeing

care
caring
uncaring

carnation
carnations

cartoonist
cartoons

cater
caterer

center
central

coast
coaster

come
comes

cool
cooler

copier
copies

corner
cornered

creep
creepy

cross
across

curl
curly

cute
cuter

dance
dancer

deep
deepen
deepened
deeper

detain
detainee

diet
dieted
dieter

direct
directions
directors
directs
indirect

dirt
dirty

disease
diseased

dive
diver

do
redo

dries
dry

donation
donors

due
overdue

eat
eaten
uneaten
eaters
eating
edible
inedible

edit
edited
editor
editors

end
ended

force
enforce

sure
ensure
insure

fan
fanning

farm
farmer

fiction
fictional

fierce
fiercely

final
finalists

firm
firmly

fit
fits
unfit

free
freed
freedom

full
fuller
fully

gain
regain

grace
gracious
disgrace

grew
grow
growth

heat
heater
reheat

hesitant
hesitate

hit
hits

ignorant
ignore

indent
indented

intend
intended

join
joints

ladies
lady

late
later

leap
leaped

list
listed
unlisted
enlist

live
liven

lose
loser
loss
lost

low
lower
lowly

mate
mating
inmate

mean
meaning
meant

medic
medical

name
named

neat
neatest

need
needed

net
Internet

nice
nicer
nicest

nose
nosier

note
notes
notice
notifies

novel
novelist

oil
oily

open
opener
reopen

operable
operate
organ
organist

paid
prepaid
repaid

parole
parolee

patriot
patriotic
patriots

pedal
pedaled

pest
pester

pin
unpin

poem
poems

polar
pole

poor
poorer
poorest

prepare
prepared

prince
princess

prove
proven
proves

pull
pulley

pure
impure

race
racer
racial
racing
racist

radio
radioed

rage
raging
outrage

rain
rainiest

read
reader
reread

rent
rental

rescue
rescuer

ride
riders
rode

right
rights

riot
rioters
riotous
riots

ripe
ripen
ripened
riper
unripe

rise
risen

romance
romantic

rose
roses
rosy

rot
rotten

run
overrun

safe
safely

sale
resale

sane
insane

scan
scanning

scare
scared
scary

scoot
scooter

score
scored

scorpion
scorpions

seal
sealed
sealer
reseal

seat
reseat

secure
insecure

seize
seized
seizure

set
preset
reset

side
aside

sing
singer
singers

sit
sitter

sleep
asleep

slow
slower

smile
smiling

social
socialist
antisocial

solo
soloist

sting
stingers

steal
stole
stolen

sun
sunnier

taco
tacos

tame
tamed

tan
tanning

tearful
tears

threw
throw

tie
tied
untie
untied
retie
retied

tiger
tigers

tight
tighter

time
timer

Titanic
titans

toast
toaster

toil
toils

tolerant
intolerant

tool
tools

tour
tourist
tours

trace
retrace

train
trained
trainee
trainer

trap
entrap

treat
treats
mistreat

troop
trooper
troops

trust
entrust

unicorn

unicorns

unite
united
reunite

use
reuse
using
reusing

virus
viruses

vote
voter
votes

write
wrote

CD-2420 Big Words for Big Kids
© Carson-Dellosa

## Other Words with Roots, Prefixes, and Suffixes Taught

Once students know and can use the roots, prefixes, and suffixes taught in *Big Words for Big Kids*, they should be able to pronounce, spell, and, in some cases, build meanings for hundreds of other words. Here are some words that students should be able to pronounce, spell, and build meanings for based on the roots, prefixes, and suffixes taught. Be a Mind Reader (p. 141) and WORDO (p. 143) games can be used to work with these words. (These words were **not** included in the lessons and are **not** in CD-2812 Big Words for Big Kids Word Card Set.)

## Roots

**act**  actively activity actualize activate activator counteract deactivate deactivation interaction overactive proactive radioactive reactivate reactivation reenactment

**appear**  appearance reappear reappearance

**bio**  biographer biology biography autobiography biographical autobiographical biological

**bright**  brightly

**class**  classier classiest classical classifier misclassify reclassify reclassification underclass underclassmen unclassified unclassifiable

**courage**  discouraged discouragement

**cover**  coverless discoverer recovery irrecoverable

**create**  creativity creatively recreate

**cred**  credibly credibility accredited discredit incredibly incredulous

**depend**  dependant dependency dependable dependability independently undependable undependability

**dic**  dictate addict addiction contradictory edict indicate indicator indication indicative predictably predictive unpredictably jurisdiction

CD-2420 Big Words for Big Kids

| | |
|---|---|
| **fec** | affect affection confection defect defective defection defector disinfect disinfectant effect effective ineffective effectively ineffectively effectiveness ineffectiveness infection perfection perfectionist imperfection proficient proficiently proficiency unaffected uninfected |
| **form** | conform conformist conformity deformed disinformation inform information informer informant informative informal informally misinform misinformation performer reformer reformation transform transformation transformer uninformed unformed unreformed formless formation formally formality formal |
| **health** | healthy healthful healthily healthiness unhealthy unhealthier unhealthful unhealthiness unhealthily |
| **jec** | conjecture dejected dejection eject ejection injector injectable interjection objective projection reject rejection subject subjective |
| **lead** | leaderless cheerleader ringleader |
| **magnet** | magnetically antimagnetic electromagnetic |
| **mis/mit** | missionary admission admissible admittedly admittance antimissile commission commit commitment committee commissary compromise dismiss dismissal emit inadmissible intermission intermittent intermittently omission permit permissive permissible remission readmission transmitted transmit transmission submit submission submissive subcommittee overcommitted |
| **nation** | nationally nationalist nationalize internationally internationalize internationalization |
| **place** | placement displace displacement misplace replacement |
| **please** | pleasurable pleasingly pleasant displeasure unpleasant |
| **port** | deportable exporter exportation important importantly importer importation importable reportedly transporter support supporter supportive unimportant |

**pon/pos**    opponent position possible posture positive poster positively composition composure counterproposal deposit depositor decompose decomposition dispose disposal disposition disposable exposition exposure impose imposition impossible oppose opposite opposition preposition propose proposal proposition repose transpose suppose supposition unexposed purposeful

**power**    empower powerlessly overpowered superpower

**press**    compression compressor decompression depressed depression depressingly antidepressant expressive expressively expressly impressively impressionist impressionistic misimpression oppress oppressive oppressively oppression oppressor repress repression repressive repressively suppress suppression

**sign**    consignment redesign designate designation ensign insignia significance insignificance reassign reassignment undersigned unsigned signify

**spec**    speculation speculative spectacularly inspection perspective prospects respect respectful disrespectful respectable respectability respective suspect suspicion  uninspected unsuspecting

**spir**    spiritual aspire aspirations conspiracy expiration inspiration perspire perspiration respiration respiratory transpire unexpired

**struct**    structure structural constructive constructively restructured reconstruction instructor instructional instruction destruction destructive obstruction obstructive superstructure unstructured unreconstructed

**tract**    attract attraction attractive attractively attractiveness unattractiveness contractor contractual contractible detract detractor distract distraction distractible extract extraction protracted

**ven**    adventure adventurous adventuress convention conventional convene eventful inventive intervene misadventure preventable preventive reconvene uneventful unpreventable unconventional venture

**vis**    advise advisor advisable envision improvise invisible invisibly invisibility provision provisional revise revision supervisor supervisory unsupervised unadvisable visionless visible visibility visualize

**weigh**    weighty weightier weightiest weightless weightlessness weightlifter counterweight unweighed

# Prefixes

**a/ad**    adventure adventurous adventuress advise advisor advisable unadvisable admission admissible admittedly admittance affect affection attract attractive attractively attractiveness unattractiveness attraction addict addiction aspire aspirations accredited

**anti**    antimagnetic antimissile antidepressant

**com/con**    commission commit commitment committee commissary compromise composition composure compression compressor confection conform conformist conformity conjecture consignment conspiracy constructive constructively contractor contractual contractible convention conventional convene

**counter/contra**    counteract counterweight counterproposal contradictory

**de**    depressed depression depressingly decompression deformed destruction destructive defect defective defection defector dejected dejection deposit depositor decompose decomposition detract detractor deactivate deactivation designate designation deportable

**dis**    dismiss dismissal dispose disposal disposition disposable displace displacement distract distraction distractible discourage discouragement disinfect disinfectant displeasure disrespectful discredit disinformation discoverer

**em/en**    empower ensign envision

**e/ex**    eject ejection emit eventful edict effect effective ineffective effectively ineffectively effectiveness ineffectiveness extract extraction exposition exposure expressive expressively expressly exporter exportation expiration (spir)

**im/in (in)**    important importantly importer importation importable impose imposition impressively impressionist impressionistic inspection inspiration instruction instructor instructional instrument instrumental inventive inform information informer informant informative indicate indicator indication indicative infection injector injectable insignia

**im/in/ir (not)**    imperfection improvise informal informally incredibly independently invisible invisibly invisibility inadmissible ineffective ineffectiveness incredulous insignificance irrecoverable

    CD-2420 Big Words for Big Kids

| | |
|---|---|
| **inter** | interview interaction interjection internationally internationalize internationalization intervene intermission intermittent intermittently |
| **mis** | misplace misinform misinformation misadventure misclassify misimpression |
| **ob/op** | objective obstruct obstruction obstructive oppress oppressive oppressively oppression oppressor oppose opposite opposition opponent |
| **per** | performer permit permissive permissible perspective perfection imperfection perfectionist perspire perspiration |
| **pre** | preview preventable preventive predictably unpredictably predictive preposition |
| **pro** | provide provision provisional improvise proactive project projection propose proposition proposal protracted proficient (fec) proficiently proficiency prospects |
| **re** | reappear recovery reappearance reclassify reclassification recreate reformer reformation reject rejection remission readmission replacement repose repression repressive repressively respect respectful disrespectful respectable respectability respective respiration respiratory reconstruction reconvene revise revision reportedly reviewer reactive reactivate reactivation reassign reassignment reconstruct restructure irrecoverable |
| **sub** | subject subjective submit submission submissive subcommittee suppress suppression support supporter supportive suppose supposition suspect suspicion |
| **super** | supervisor supervisory superstructure superpower |
| **trans** | transporter transmission transform transformation transformer transpose transpire |
| **un** | unaffected unattractive unexposed uneventful unexpired unimportant uninfected unclassified unclassifiable unpleasant unformed unreformed uninformed undependable unhealthy unhealthier unhealthful unhealthiness unsigned uninspected unsuspecting unpreventable unsupervised unweighed unadvisable unstructured unreconstructed unconventional unpredictably |

| | |
|---|---|
| **over** | overpowered overreacted overactive overcommitted |
| **under** | underclass underclassmen undersigned |

## Suffixes

| | |
|---|---|
| **er/est** | brighter classier classiest unhealthier weightier weightiest |
| **ize** | visualize nationalize internationalize actualize |
| **ify** | magnify signify reclassify misclassify |
| **ate** | dictate activate deactivate reactivate designate indicate recreate speculate |
| **less** | coverless formless leaderless weightless visionless |
| **ful** | healthful unhealthful purposeful |
| **able/ible** | respectable dependable preventable unpreventable advisable unadvisable unclassifiable injectable deportable importable transportable retractable predictably unpredictably pleasurable disposable irrecoverable admissible inadmissible permissible distractible visible invisible contractible possible impossible |
| **ly** | admittedly incredibly independently intermittently invisibly reportedly actively brightly creatively credibly incredibly dependably predictably unpredictably formally informally healthily unhealthily nationally internationally pleasingly importantly powerlessly depressingly impressively expressively expressly repressively oppressively spectacularly constructively proficiently effectively ineffectively positively magnetically |
| **er/or** | transformer exporter importer informer performer reformer reviewer supporter transporter discoverer biographer classifier cheerleader ringleader weightlifter actor advisor compressor contractor depositor detractor instructor indicator supervisor injector defector activator oppressor |
| **ist** | conformist perfectionist nationalist impressionist |
| **ess** | adventuress |

CD-2420 Big Words for Big Kids

**sion/tion**    admission commission intermission transmission submission remission readmission oppression compression decompression depression repression suppression misimpression envision provision provisional revision reclassification affection confection defection infection perfection imperfection perfectionist attraction distraction extraction dictation addiction indication jurisdiction position composition decomposition disposition exposition imposition proposition supposition opposition preposition convention conventional unconventional destruction instruction instructional reconstruction dejection ejection interjection projection rejection obstruction expiration inspiration perspiration respiration aspirations inspection formation information misinformation reformation transformation disinformation interaction activation deactivation reactivation internationalize internationalization designation importation exportation speculation

**ance/ence**    admittance appearance reappearance significance insignificance

**ment**    discouragement placement displacement replacement commitment instrument instrumental reenactment reassignment

**ness**    healthiness unhealthiness weightlessness effectiveness ineffectiveness attractiveness

**ity/y**    activity creativity credibility conformity visibility invisibility respectability dependability undependability formality respiratory contradictory dependency conspiracy recovery supervisory biology biography autobiography commissary missionary

**sure/ture**    composure displeasure exposure adventure misadventure conjecture superstructure structure restructure unstructured venture posture

**ant/ent**    pleasant unpleasant unimportant important importantly disinfectant informant antidepressant dependant independently intermittent intermittently proficient proficiently opponent

**al**    classical contractual conventional unconventional dismissal disposal instructional instrumental informal formality provisional proposal counterproposal biographical autobiographical biological spiritual signal structural

| | |
|---|---|
| **ive** | attractive attractively unattractive constructive constructively destructive obstructive effective ineffective effectively ineffectively defective expressive expressively impressively repressive oppressive oppressively inventive preventive informative perspective actively overactive proactive reactive radioactive respective subjective objective creatively predictive indicative permissive submissive supportive positive speculative |
| **ous** | adventurous incredulous |
| **ic** | antimagnetic electromagnetic impressionistic |

## Other Common Words with Prefixes and Suffixes

Here are some other common words that begin or end with the prefixes and suffixes taught. Be a Mind Reader (p. 141) and WORDO (p. 143) games can be used to work with these words. (These words were **not** included in the lessons and are **not** in CD-2812 Big Words for Big Kids Word Card Set.)

## Prefixes:

### a/ad (note doubling of letters: f, g, l, n, p, r, s, t)

addresses adjustor adjustment administer administration admirer admirable admiration advancing advancement advantage advantageous advertise advertisement advocate affirmation affirmative afflicted affliction aggravate aggression allocation allowance annexation announcer announcement appointment apprehend apprehensive approach approachable approving approval arrangement arrested assisted assistant assistance assuming assumption attaches attachment attacker attempted attending attendant attendance attention attentive

| | |
|---|---|
| **anti** | antiwar antibody antifreeze antiseptic antitrust |
| **con/com** | commander commandment communities communicate communication comparative comparatively complexity companionship competitive compassion   computer combustion compartment commotion conductor confusion conclusion conjunction conviction conversion conviction confirmation contagious confession convulsion conservative consistently constitution congratulations confederation confederacy contamination |
| **contra** | contraband contraception |
| **de** | department description descriptive departure defensive detective |

CD-2420 Big Words for Big Kids    © Carson-Dellosa

detection detention detachment democracy democratic demoralize debatable degenerate deteriorate

**dis**
disadvantage disapproval disappointment disagreement disagreeable disorganized disillusioned dislocated disorderly disoriented disarmament dishonesty disloyalty disqualify dissatisfied disproportionate dishonorable disobedience disability disruption disgraceful distrustful discomfort discontinued disenfranchise

**en**
enable enjoyment enjoyable entertainment endurance engagement enrollment enchantment encircle enclosure endanger enlargement enfranchise enlighten enraged

**e/ex**
evaluate eruption erosion evasion evasive eviction emotional evaporation emancipate enunciate evacuation expansion explorer exploration exaggerate excellent expensive exclamation explosion excitement extension extortion expedition execution executioner explanation experiment expert external

**im/in (in)**
improvement impulsive implant immersion immigrant immigration imprisonment internal insurance influential invasion inflation induction inscription investigator

**il/im/in/ir (not)**
illegal illogical illegitimate impurities improper impatiently impatience immoral immortal imperfection immature imprudent impractical impersonal imperceptible incomplete indirect incorrect injustice inexpensive inequalities incompetent intolerable inexperienced indescribable inoperable irregular irrational irresponsible irreversible

**inter**
interception intersection interference interruption interpretation intermediate interchangeable

**mis**
misuse mistake misunderstand mismanaged misfortune miscarriage misbehave misfit misguided misspelled mistrustful mistreatment

**ob (note doubling of letter f)**
obstinate obnoxious obsolete offend offensive

**per**
percussion percentage perception perceptible perfume permanent perjury perseverance persistence persuasion

**pre**
preceding predominant previous prefabricated preference prejudiced

premature premonition preparation prescription prefixes

**pro**
proceed procedure procession proclaim proclamation produce production professor professional progressive promotion promoter protection protective provocative profit profitable prophet

**re**
rebound rebellious receive recognize recognition recorder reduction reflection refreshments refrigerator relationship relatives relaxation remember remembrance remorseful remorseless removal renewal renovations reorganize repetition repetitious repercussions requirements research resistance responsible responsibilities retaliation retaliatory retreat retrieve revenge reversible reusable

**trans**
transatlantic transcontinental transcend transfer transcript transition transparent transplant translation translator

**tele**
telephone telescope telescopic telepathy telethon

**sub (suf/sup/sus):**
subcontract subconscious subway submarine substitute submerge subscribe subscription substandard subtitles subservient subversive subtropical suffixes supplies supplants suspend suspension sustain

**super**
superman supermarket supersonic superior superhuman superficial superintendent superstitious

**over**
overjoyed overhead overalls overlook overhaul overkill overnight

**under**
underground underwear underestimate underdeveloped undertaking understanding underline undergraduate underhanded underage

**un**
unwritten unbeaten unbroken unbelievable unhappiness unapproachable unbreakable uncertain uncomfortable unforgettable unfriendly unfortunately unsuccessful unusual unreliable unlovable unending

# Suffixes:

**er/est**
easier easiest greater greatest colder coldest hotter hottest funnier funniest

**en**
mistaken unbroken unbeaten unwritten enlighten

**less**
hopeless motionless meaningless remorseless

**ful**
careful thoughtful beautiful distrustful mistrustful disgraceful unsuccessful

**able/ible**
admirable approachable debatable dishonorable enjoyable indescribable

inoperable  profitable  reusable  unapproachable  unbreakable
uncomfortable  unforgettable  unreliable  sensible  unbelievable  perceptible
imperceptible  reversible  irreversible  responsible  irresponsible

**tion/sion**  administration admiration affirmation affliction allocation annexation
assumption attention communication combustion commotion conjunction
conviction confirmation constitution congratulations confederation
contamination contraception description detection detention disproportionate
disruption eruption eviction emotional evaporation evacuation exploration
exclamation extortion expedition execution executioner explanation
immigration inflation induction inscription imperfection interception
intersection interruption interpretation perception premonition prescription
proclamation production promotion protection recognition reduction
reflection relationship relaxation renovations repetition retaliation transition
translation subscription aggression compassion confusion conclusion
conversion confession convulsion disillusioned erosion evasion expansion
explosion extension immersion invasion percussion persuasion
procession professional repercussions suspension

**ly**  suddenly easily ordinarily comparatively consistently disorderly impatiently
unfriendly unfortunately

**er/or**  admirer announcer attacker commander computer explorer executioner
recorder prisoner governor investigator generator adjustor conductor
professor refrigerator translator

**ist**  scientist specialist journalist lobbyist

**ess**  waitress hostess empress countess

**ance/ence**  allowance assistance attendance endurance insurance perseverance
remembrance resistance disobedience impatience interference
persistence preference

**ment**  adjustment advancement advertisement announcement appointment
arrangement attachment commandment compartment department
detachment disappointment disagreement disarmament enjoyment
entertainment engagement enrollment enchantment enlargement
excitement experiment improvement imprisonment mistreatment
permanent refreshments requirements

**ness**  weakness kindness friendliness happiness unhappiness

**ity/y**  complexity disloyalty disability confederacy democracy dishonesty perjury telepathy

**ant/ent**  assistant attendant immigrant predominant transparent excellent incompetent subservient superintendent imprudent permanent

**al**  unusual political colonial emotional professional approval disapproval internal influential immoral immortal impractical impersonal irrational illegal illogical removal transcontinental superficial subtropical

**ive**  affirmative apprehensive attentive comparative comparatively competitive conservative descriptive defensive detective evasive expensive impulsive inexpensive progressive protective provocative relative subversive

**ous**  dangerous hazardous mysterious strenuous advantageous contagious previous rebellious repetitious subconscious superstitious

**ic**  democratic antiseptic supersonic telescopic transatlantic

**ify**  simplify testify specify qualify disqualify

**ize**  criticize capitalize apologize maximize recognize reorganize

**ate**  generate nominate evaluate advocate aggravate communicate degenerate deteriorate emancipate enunciate estimate underestimate exaggerate

**sure/ture**  enclosure departure immature premature legislature

**ship**  leadership sportsmanship companionship relationship

# Be a Mind Reader

Be a Mind Reader is a favorite Word Wall review activity. In this game, the teacher thinks of a word from the Word Wall, and then gives five clues to that word. Choose a word and write it on a scrap of paper, but do not let the students see which word you have written. Have students number their papers from one to five, and tell them that you are going to see who can read your mind and figure out which of the Word Wall words you have written on your paper. Tell them you will give them five clues. By the fifth clue, everyone should guess the word, but if they read your mind they might get it before the fifth clue.

For your first clue, tell the students, "It's one of the words on the wall." When you have more than 40 words, narrow it down a little by saying, "It's in the first half of the alphabet (A-M)," or "It's in the last half of the alphabet (N-Z)." Each succeeding clue should narrow down what the word can be. As you give each clue, students write the word they believe the chosen word to be next to each number. If a new clue fits the word a student has written for a previous clue, the student writes that word again by the next numbers. If the new clue rules out the word the student has chosen, then the student chooses another word. By clue five, you should have narrowed down the word to just one choice. After you have given the fifth and final clue, show the students the word you wrote on your scratch paper and say, "I know you all have the word next to number five, but who has it on number four? Number three? Number two? Number one?" Usually, someone guesses the word on the first or second clue. Express amazement that they "read your mind!"

Here are a few examples with the clues and a few students' papers.

Assume the following words are on the wall:

| | | | | | | | |
|---|---|---|---|---|---|---|---|
| brighten | creatures | demagnetize | magnetic | overweight | powerful | recreation | underweight |
| brightest | create | displeased | | | powerfully | | |
| brightness | | | | | pleasures | | |
| | | | | | powerless | | |

1. It's one of the Word Wall words.
2. It has 8 or more letters
3. It begins with a **p**.
4. The root word is **power**.
5. It ends with the suffix **less**.

Student examples:

| | | |
|---|---|---|
| 1. brightness | 1. create | 1. powerless |
| 2. brightness | 2. creatures | 2. powerless |
| 3. powerless | 3. pleasures | 3. powerless |
| 4. powerless | 4. powerful | 4. powerless |
| 5. powerless | 5. powerless | 5. powerless (He read your mind!) |

Now assume all 100 words are on the wall.

1. It's in the first half of the alphabet (**A-M**).
2. It begins with a **d**.
3. It begins with the prefix **dis**.
4. It ends with **ed**.
5. It means **the opposite of encouraged**.

Student examples:

| 1. actresses | 1. conspirators | 1. dictatorship |
|---|---|---|
| 2. discouraged | 2. depressing | 2. dictatorship |
| 3. discouraged | 3. discovery | 3. displeased |
| 4. discouraged | 4. displeased | 4. displeased |
| 5. discouraged | 5. discouraged | 5. discouraged |

Be a Mind Reader can be used to review any displayed words. You can use the other words from the Making Words lessons or words from any of the lists of words listed under Review and Extension activities. It is important to display the words in some way. If you are not using the words on a Word Wall, write them on index cards and display them in a pocket chart or along the chalk ledge.

# WORDO

WORDO is a variation of the ever-popular Bingo game. Students love it and don't even realize they are getting practice reading and writing words. All you need to play WORDO are some sheets of paper on which 25 blocks have been drawn and some small pieces of paper or objects to cover words as students fill in the blocks. You can make your own WORDO sheets or copy the reproducible WORDO sheet on page 144.

You can use WORDO to review the Word Wall words or to practice extension words. For each WORDO game, choose 24 words. Then, tell the students the word and have them watch while you write it on an index card. They then choose the block on their sheets where they choose to put it. When all 24 words are called out, everyone should have the same 24 words on their sheets—but in different places.

To play the game, the caller shuffles the index cards and calls out words one at a time. Students chant the spelling of the word and then cover the word on their WORDO sheet. The first person to cover a row of words in any direction wins WORDO. The winner reads the words covered to be sure that these words were called. Then, check to see that all words in the winning row were spelled correctly. (If a student has misspelled a word in the winning row, he cannot win and play continues.) When you have a winner, everyone can clear their sheets and play again.

WORDO can be used to review Word Wall words or to help students focus on extension words. Students pay more attention to the prefix and suffix patterns if you call words that fit a few of the patterns. From the extension lists, you could choose 24 words that have the suffix **tion** or **sion**, 24 words that begin with the "opposite" prefixes: **un**, **in**, and **dis**, or 24 words that have the Latin roots **struct**, **tract**, or **cred**. The possibilities are almost endless. WORDO can help students develop fluency with the key words on the Word Wall and improve their ability to combine roots, prefixes, and suffixes to spell hundreds of other words.

# WORDO

| W | O | R | D | O |
|---|---|---|---|---|
|   |   |   |   |   |
|   |   |   |   |   |
|   |   | FREE |   |   |
|   |   |   |   |   |
|   |   |   |   |   |

 CD-2420 Big Words for Big Kids

# Making Words Take-Home Sheet

across

act

acting

action

actions

active

actor

actors

actress

actresses

admit

agree

agreement

airport

alien

alienation

alter

alteration

altered

anger

angriest

antibiotics

antisocial

appear

appeared

argue

argument

arm

armful

arms

arson

arsonist

art

artist

artistic

aside

asleep

assign

assignment

be

being

biologist

biologists

bionic

bit

bite

bled

bleed

blend

blender

boss

bossy

botanic

botanist

bred

breed

bright

brighten

brightest

brightness

build

call

caller

camp

camper

canoe

canoeing

care

caring

carnation

carnations

cartoonist

cartoons

cater

caterer

center

central

class

classic

classification

classify

classy

coast

coaster

come

comes

compose

composers

compress

conspirator

conspirators

conspire

conspired

conspires

construct

construction

contraction

contracts

contradict

contradictions

cool

cooler

copier

copies

corner

cornered
courage
courageous
courageously
cover
covered
create
creates
creation
creative
creator
creatures
credible
creditors
credits
creep
creepy
cross
curl
curly
cute
cuter
dance
dancer
deal
dealer
dealership
declassify
deep
deepen
deepened
deeper
deform
deformity
demagnetize
depend
dependence
dependent
deport

depress
depressing
design
designer
destruct
destructible
detain
detainee
dictator
dictators
dictatorship
diet
dieted
dieter
direct
directions
directors
directs
dirt
dirty
disappear
disappearance
discouraged
discover
discovery
disease
diseased
disgrace
displeased
distract
distraction
dive
diver
do
donation
donors
dries
dry
due

eat
eaten
eaters
eating
edible
edit
edited
editor
editors
emission
enact
encourage
encouragement
encouraging
end
ended
enforce
enlist
ensure
entrap
entrust
event
export
exportable
expose
express
expression
fan
fanning
farm
farmer
fiction
fictional
fierce
fiercely
final
finalists
firm
firmly

fit
fits
force
form
formal
format
formed
formula
formulates
free
freed
freedom
full
fuller
fully
gain
grace
gracious
grew
grow
growth
heal
healer
health
healthier
healthiest
heat
heater
hesitant
hesitate
hit
hits
ignorant
ignore
imperfect
imperfectly
import
importance
impossibility

impossibly
impress
impression
impressive
impure
inactive
incredible
indent
indented
independence
independent
indestructible
indirect
inedible
infect
infectious
infects
inject
inmate
insane
insecure
insignificant
inspect
inspector
inspectors
inspire
inspired
inspires
insure
intend
intended
interact
interactive
international
Internet
intervention
intolerant
invent
invention

inventor
irreplaceable
join
joints
ladies
lady
late
later
lead
leader
leadership
leap
leaped
list
listed
live
liven
lose
loser
loss
lost
low
lower
lowly
magnet
magnetic
magnetize
magnets
mate
mating
mean
meaning
meant
medic
medical
misdeal
misdealing
mislead
misleading

misplaced
mission
mistreat
name
named
nation
national
nationalities
nations
neat
neatest
need
needed
net
nice
nicer
nicest
nose
nosier
note
notes
notice
notifies
novel
novelist
object
objections
oil
oily
omit
omits
open
opener
operable
operate
organ
organist
outrage
overrun

overdue
overweight
paid
parole
parolee
patriot
patriotic
patriots
pedal
pedaled
perfect
perfectly
perform
performance
permission
pest
pester
pin
place
placed
places
please
pleasures
poem
poems
polar
pole
poor
poorer
poorest
port
portable
pose
possibility
possibly
post
poster
power
powerful

powerfully
powerless
predict
predictable
predictions
prepaid
prepare
prepared
preset
press
pressed
pressing
pressure
pressured
pressurized
prevent
prevention
prince
princess
project
projectors
promise
promises
prove
proven
proves
pull
pulley
pure
race
racer
racial
racing
racist
radio
radioed
rage
raging
rain

rainiest

react

reaction

reactions

reactor

read

reader

readmit

reappeared

rebuild

recall

recover

recreation

redesign

redo

reform

reformed

regain

reheat

remit

rent

rental

reopen

repaid

replace

report

reporters

repress

reread

resale

rescue

rescuer

reseal

reseat

reset

resign

resignation

retie

retied

retrace

retract

retraction

reunite

reuse

reusing

review

ride

riders

right

rights

riot

rioters

riotous

riots

ripe

ripen

ripened

riper

rise

risen

rode

romance

romantic

rose

roses

rosy

rot

rotten

run

safe

safely

sale

sane

scan

scanning

scare

scared

scary

scoot

scooter

score

scored

scorpion

scorpions

seal

sealed

sealer

seat

secure

seize

seized

seizure

set

side

sign

signal

signaled

signature

signed

signer

significant

signs

sing

singer

singers

sit

sitter

sleep

slow

slower

smile

smiling

social

socialist

solo

soloist

spectator

CD-2420 Big Words for Big Kids

spectators
steal
sting
stingers
stole
stolen
subtract
subtraction
sun
sunnier
supervision
sure
taco
tacos
tame
tamed
tan
tanning
tearful
tears
television
threw
throw
tie
tied
tiger
tigers
tight
tighter
time
timer
titanic
titans
toast
toaster
toil
toils
tolerant
tool

tools
tour
tourist
tours
trace
traction
tractor
train
trained
trainee
trainer
transact
transaction
transmit
transmitted
transport
transportation
trap
treat
treats
troop
trooper
troops
trust
unaltered
uncaring
uncovered
undercover
underweight
uneaten
unfit
unhealthiest
unicorn
unicorns
unimpressive
uninspired
unite
united
unlisted

unpin
unpredictable
unripe
untie
untied
use
using
view
virus
viruses
vision
visors
vote
voter
votes
weigh
weighed
weight
write
wrote

# Take-Home Word Wall
## Lesson 5

| A a | G g | P p |
|---|---|---|
| **B b**<br>brighten<br>brightest<br>brightness | H h | |
| | I i | Q q |
| C c | | R r |
| | | |
| | | S s |
| | J j | |
| **D d**<br>demagnetize | K k | T t |
| | L l | |
| | **M m**<br>magnetic | U u |
| E e | | |
| | N n | V v |
| | | W w |
| F f | O o | X x    Y y    Z z |

CD-2420 Big Words for Big Kids    © Carson-Dellosa

# Take-Home Word Wall
## Lesson 10

| A a | G g | P p |
|---|---|---|
| | | powerful |
| | | powerfully |
| | H h | powerless |
| **B b** | | |
| brighten | I i | |
| brightest | | Q q |
| brightness | | R r |
| **C c** | | |
| | | |
| | | |
| | | S s |
| | J j | |
| | K k | |
| **D d** | | T t |
| demagnetize | L l | |
| | **M m** | **U u** |
| | magnetic | underweight |
| E e | | |
| | N n | V v |
| | | W w |
| F f | O o | X x    Y y    Z z |
| | overweight | |

# Take-Home Word Wall
## Lesson 15

| A a | G g | P p |
|---|---|---|
| | | powerful |
| | | powerfully |
| | | powerless |
| **B b** | **H h** | **pleasures** |
| brighten | | |
| brightest | **I i** | **Q q** |
| brightness | | |
| **C c** | | **R r** |
| creatures | | recreation |
| creator | | |
| | **J j** | **S s** |
| **D d** | **K k** | |
| demagnetize | | **T t** |
| displeased | **L l** | |
| | **M m** | |
| | magnetic | **U u** |
| **E e** | | underweight |
| | **N n** | |
| | | **V v** |
| | | **W w** |
| **F f** | **O o** | |
| | overweight | X x    Y y    Z z |

CD-2420 Big Words for Big Kids

# Take-Home Word Wall
## Lesson 20

### A a
actors
actresses

### B b
brighten
brightest
brightness

### C c
creatures
creator

### D d
demagnetize
displeased

### E e

### F f

### G g

### H h

### I i
interactive

### J j

### K k

### L l

### M m
magnetic

### N n

### O o
overweight

### P p
powerful
powerfully
powerless
pleasures

### Q q

### R r
recreation
reactions

### S s

### T t
transaction

### U u
underweight

### V v

### W w

### X x    Y y    Z z

# Take-Home Word Wall
## Lesson 25

**A a**
actors
actresses

**B b**
brighten
brightest
brightness

**C c**
creatures
creator

**D d**
demagnetize
displeased
**discovery**
**disappearance**

**E e**

**F f**

**G g**

**H h**

**I i**
interactive

**J j**

**K k**

**L l**

**M m**
magnetic

**N n**

**O o**
overweight

**P p**
powerful
powerfully
powerless
pleasures

**Q q**

**R r**
recreation
reactions
**reappeared**

**S s**

**T t**
transaction

**U u**
underweight
**uncovered**
**undercover**

**V v**

**W w**

**X x**　　**Y y**　　**Z z**

　CD-2420 Big Words for Big Kids　© Carson-Dellosa

# Take-Home Word Wall
## Lesson 30

**A a**

actors
actresses

**B b**

brighten
brightest
brightness

**C c**

creatures
creator
**courageous**
**courageously**

**D d**

demagnetize
displeased
discovery
disappearance
**discouraged**

**E e**

**encouraging**
**encouragement**

**F f**

**G g**

**H h**

**I i**

interactive

**J j**

**K k**

**L l**

**M m**

magnetic

**N n**

**O o**

overweight

**P p**

powerful
powerfully
powerless
pleasures

**Q q**

**R r**

recreation
reactions
reappeared

**S s**

**T t**

transaction

**U u**

underweight
uncovered
undercover

**V v**

**W w**

**X x**        **Y y**        **Z z**

CD-2420 Big Words for Big Kids

# Take-Home Word Wall
## Lesson 35

### A a
actors
actresses
assignment

### B b
brighten
brightest
brightness

### C c
creatures
creator
courageous
courageously

### D d
demagnetize
displeased
discovery
disappearance
discouraged

### E e
encouraging
encouragement

### F f

### G g

### H h

### I i
interactive
insignificant

### J j

### K k

### L l

### M m
magnetic

### N n

### O o
overweight

### P p
powerful
powerfully
powerless
pleasures

### Q q

### R r
recreation
reactions
reappeared
resignation

### S s
signature
significant

### T t
transaction

### U u
underweight
uncovered
undercover

### V v

### W w

### X x    Y y    Z z

# Take-Home Word Wall
## Lesson 40

### A a
actors
actresses
assignment

### B b
brighten
brightest
brightness

### C c
creatures
creator
courageous
courageously

### D d
demagnetize
displeased
discovery
disappearance
discouraged
dealership

### E e
encouraging
encouragement

### F f

### G g

### H h

### I i
interactive
insignificant
irreplaceable

### J j

### K k

### L l
leadership

### M m
magnetic
misplaced
misleading

### N n

### O o
overweight

### P p
powerful
powerfully
powerless
pleasures

### Q q

### R r
recreation
reactions
reappeared
resignation

### S s
signature
significant

### T t
transaction

### U u
underweight
uncovered
undercover

### V v

### W w

### X x        Y y        Z z

# Take-Home Word Wall
## Lesson 45

**A a**

actors
actresses
assignment

**B b**

brighten
brightest
brightness

**C c**

creatures
creator
courageous
courageously

**D d**

demagnetize
displeased
discovery
disappearance
discouraged
dealership

**E e**

encouraging
encouragement

**F f**

**G g**

**H h**

**I i**

interactive
insignificant
irreplaceable
independent
independence
international

**J j**

**K k**

**L l**

leadership

**M m**

magnetic
misplaced
misleading

**N n**

national
nationalities

**O o**

overweight

**P p**

powerful
powerfully
powerless
pleasures

**Q q**

**R r**

recreation
reactions
reappeared
resignation

**S s**

signature
significant

**T t**

transaction

**U u**

underweight
uncovered
undercover

**V v**

**W w**

**X x    Y y    Z z**

CD-2420 Big Words for Big Kids

# Take-Home Word Wall
## Lesson 50

### A a
actors
actresses
assignment

### B b
brighten
brightest
brightness

### C c
creatures
creator
courageous
courageously
classic
classification

### D d
demagnetize      declassify
displeased
discovery
disappearance
discouraged
dealership

### E e
encouraging
encouragement

### F f

### G g

### H h
healthier

### I i
interactive
insignificant
irreplaceable
independent
independence
international

### J j

### K k

### L l
leadership

### M m
magnetic
misplaced
misleading

### N n
national
nationalities

### O o
overweight

### P p
powerful
powerfully
powerless
pleasures

### Q q

### R r
recreation
reactions
reappeared
resignation

### S s
signature
significant

### T t
transaction

### U u
underweight
uncovered
undercover
unhealthiest

### V v

### W w

### X x          Y y          Z z

# Take-Home Word Wall
## Lesson 55

### A a
actors
actresses
assignment

### B b
brighten
brightest
brightness

### C c
creatures
creator
courageous
courageously
classic
classification

### D d
demagnetize    declassify
displeased    depressing
discovery
disappearance
discouraged
dealership

### E e
encouraging
encouragement
expression

### F f

### G g

### H h
healthier

### I i
interactive
insignificant
irreplaceable
independent
independence
international

### J j

### K k

### L l
leadership

### M m
magnetic
misplaced
misleading

### N n
national
nationalities

### O o
overweight

### P p
powerful
powerfully
powerless
pleasures
pressurized

### Q q

### R r
recreation    repress
reactions
reappeared
resignation

### S s
signature
significant

### T t
transaction

### U u
underweight    unimpressive
uncovered
undercover
unhealthiest

### V v

### W w

### X x    Y y    Z z

CD-2420 Big Words for Big Kids    © Carson-Dellosa

# Take-Home Word Wall
## Lesson 60

### A a
actors
actresses
assignment

### B b
brighten
brightest
brightness

### C c
creatures
creator
courageous
courageously
classic
classification

### D d
demagnetize    declassify
displeased    depressing
discovery    **deformity**
disappearance
discouraged
dealership

### E e
encouraging
encouragement
expression

### F f
**formal**
**formulates**

### G g

### H h
healthier

### I i
interactive
insignificant
irreplaceable
independent
independence
international

### J j

### K k

### L l
leadership

### M m
magnetic
misplaced
misleading

### N n
national
nationalities

### O o
overweight

### P p
powerful
powerfully
powerless
pleasures
pressurized
**performance**

### Q q

### R r
recreation    repress
reactions    **reformed**
reappeared
resignation

### S s
signature
significant

### T t
transaction

### U u
underweight    unimpressive
uncovered
undercover
unhealthiest

### V v

### W w

### X x    Y y    Z z

© Carson-Dellosa     CD-2420 Big Words for Big Kids     163

## A a
actors
actresses
assignment

## B b
brighten
brightest
brightness

## C c
creatures
creator
courageous
courageously
classic
classification

## D d
demagnetize      declassify
displeased       depressing
discovery        deformity
disappearance
discouraged
dealership

## E e
encouraging
encouragement
expression
exportable

## F f
formal
formulates

## G g

## H h
healthier

## I i
interactive
insignificant
irreplaceable
independent
independence
international
importance

## J j

## K k

## L l
leadership

## M m
magnetic
misplaced
misleading

## N n
national
nationalities

## O o
overweight

## P p
portable
powerful
powerfully
powerless
pleasures
pressurized
performance

## Q q

## R r
recreation       repress
reactions        reformed
reappeared       reporters
resignation

## S s
signature
significant

## T t
transaction
transportation

## U u
underweight   unimpressive
uncovered
undercover
unhealthiest

## V v

## W w

## X x        Y y        Z z

CD-2420 Big Words for Big Kids
© Carson-Dellosa

# Take-Home Word Wall
## Lesson 70

### A a
actors
actresses
assignment

### B b
brighten
brightest
brightness

### C c
creatures      contradictions
creator
courageous
courageously
classic
classification

### D d
demagnetize   declassify
displeased    depressing
discovery     deformity
disappearance  dictator
discouraged   dictatorship
dealership

### E e
encouraging
encouragement
expression
exportable

### F f
formal
formulates

### G g

### H h
healthier

### I i
interactive
insignificant
irreplaceable
independent
independence
international
importance

### J j

### K k

### L l
leadership

### M m
magnetic
misplaced
misleading

### N n
national
nationalities

### O o
overweight

### P p
powerful       portable
powerfully     predictions
powerless
pleasures
pressurized
performance

### Q q

### R r
recreation    repress
reactions     reformed
reappeared    reporters
resignation

### S s
signature
significant

### T t
transaction
transportation

### U u
underweight   unimpressive
uncovered     unpredictable
undercover
unhealthiest

### V v

### W w

### X x      Y y      Z z

# Take-Home Word Wall
## Lesson 75

### A a
actors
actresses
assignment

### B b
brighten
brightest
brightness

### C c
creatures     contradictions
creator     composers
courageous
courageously
classic
classification

### D d
demagnetize     declassify
displeased     depressing
discovery     deformity
disappearance     dictator
discouraged     dictatorship
dealership

### E e
encouraging
encouragement
expression
exportable
emission

### F f
formal
formulates

### G g

### H h
healthier

### I i
interactive
insignificant
irreplaceable
independent
independence
international
importance
impossibility

### J j

### K k

### L l
leadership

### M m
magnetic
misplaced
misleading

### N n
national
nationalities

### O o
overweight

### P p
powerful     portable
powerfully     predictions
powerless     permission
pleasures
pressurized
performance

### Q q

### R r
recreation     repress
reactions     reformed
reappeared     reporters
resignation

### S s
signature
significant

### T t
transaction
transportation
transmitted

### U u
underweight     unimpressive
uncovered     unpredictable
undercover
unhealthiest

### V v

### W w

### X x     Y y     Z z

CD-2420 Big Words for Big Kids     © Carson-Dellosa

# Take-Home Word Wall
## Lesson 80

### A a
actors
actresses
assignment

### B b
brighten
brightest
brightness

### C c
creatures          contradictions
creator            composers
courageous
courageously
classic
classification

### D d
demagnetize        declassify
displeased         depressing
discovery          deformity
disappearance      dictator
discouraged        dictatorship
dealership

### E e
encouraging
encouragement
expression
exportable
emission

### F f
formal
formulates

### G g

### H h
healthier

### I i
interactive        **intervention**
insignificant      **inventor**
irreplaceable      **inspectors**
independent
independence
international
importance
impossibility

### J j

### K k

### L l
leadership

### M m
magnetic
misplaced
misleading

### N n
national
nationalities

### O o
overweight

### P p
powerful           portable
powerfully         predictions
powerless          permission
pleasures          **prevention**
pressurized
performance

### Q q

### R r
recreation         repress
reactions          reformed
reappeared         reporters
resignation

### S s
signature
significant
**spectators**

### T t
transaction
transportation
transmitted

### U u
underweight        unimpressive
uncovered          unpredictable
undercover
unhealthiest

### V v

### W w

### X x          Y y          Z z

# Take-Home Word Wall
## Lesson 85

### A a
actors
actresses
assignment

### B b
brighten
brightest
brightness

### C c
creatures        contradictions
creator          composers
courageous
courageously
classic
classification

### D d
demagnetize      declassify
displeased       depressing
discovery        deformity
disappearance    dictator
discouraged      dictatorship
dealership

### E e
encouraging
encouragement
expression
exportable
emission

### F f
formal
formulates

### G g

### H h
healthier

### I i
interactive      intervention
insignificant    inventor
irreplaceable    inspectors
independent
independence
international
importance
impossibility

### J j

### K k

### L l
leadership

### M m
magnetic
misplaced
misleading

### N n
national
nationalities

### O o
overweight

### P p
powerful         portable
powerfully       predictions
powerless        permission
pleasures        prevention
pressurized
performance

### Q q

### R r
recreation       repress
reactions        reformed
reappeared       reporters
resignation      retraction

### S s
signature        supervision
significant      subtraction
spectators

### T t
transaction      television
transportation   tractor
transmitted

### U u
underweight      unimpressive
uncovered        unpredictable
undercover
unhealthiest

### V v

### W w

### X x        Y y        Z z

   CD-2420 Big Words for Big Kids

# Take-Home Word Wall
## Lesson 90

### A a
actors
actresses
assignment

### B b
brighten
brightest
brightness

### C c
creatures        contradictions
creator          composers
courageous       conspirators
courageously
classic
classification

### D d
demagnetize      declassify
displeased       depressing
discovery        deformity
disappearance    dictator
discouraged      dictatorship
dealership

### E e
encouraging
encouragement
expression
exportable
emission

### F f
formal
formulates

### G g

### H h
healthier

### I i
interactive      intervention
insignificant    inventor
irreplaceable    inspectors
independent      inject
independence
international
importance
impossibility

### J j

### K k

### L l
leadership

### M m
magnetic
misplaced
misleading

### N n
national
nationalities

### O o
overweight       objections

### P p
powerful         portable
powerfully       predictions
powerless        permission
pleasures        prevention
pressurized      projectors
performance

### Q q

### R r
recreation       repress
reactions        reformed
reappeared       reporters
resignation      retraction

### S s
signature        supervision
significant      subtraction
spectators

### T t
transaction      television
transportation   tractor
transmitted

### U u
underweight      unimpressive
uncovered        unpredictable
undercover       uninspired
unhealthiest

### V v

### W w

### X x        Y y        Z z

# Take-Home Word Wall
## Lesson 95

### A a
actors
actresses
assignment

### B b
brighten
brightest
brightness

### C c
creatures    contradictions
creator    composers
courageous    conspirators
courageously    construction
classic
classification

### D d
demagnetize    declassify
displeased    depressing
discovery    deformity
disappearance    dictator
discouraged    dictatorship
dealership

### E e
encouraging
encouragement
expression
exportable
emission

### F f
formal
formulates

### G g

### H h
healthier

### I i
interactive    intervention
insignificant    inventor
irreplaceable    inspectors
independent    inject
independence    infectious
international    imperfectly
importance    indestructible
impossibility

### J j

### K k

### L l
leadership

### M m
magnetic
misplaced
misleading

### N n
national
nationalities

### O o
overweight    objections

### P p
powerful    portable
powerfully    predictions
powerless    permission
pleasures    prevention
pressurized    projectors
performance    perfectly

### Q q

### R r
recreation    repress
reactions    reformed
reappeared    reporters
resignation    retraction

### S s
signature    supervision
significant    subtraction
spectators

### T t
transaction    television
transportation    tractor
transmitted

### U u
underweight    unimpressive
uncovered    unpredictable
undercover    uninspired
unhealthiest

### V v

### W w

### X x    Y y    Z z

CD-2420 Big Words for Big Kids

# Take-Home Word Wall
## Lesson 100

### A a
actors
actresses
assignment
antibiotics

### B b
brighten
brightest
brightness

biologists
bionic

### C c
creatures        contradictions
creator          composers
courageous       conspirators
courageously     construction
classic          creditors
classification

### D d
demagnetize      declassify
displeased       depressing
discovery        deformity
disappearance    dictator
discouraged      dictatorship
dealership

### E e
encouraging
encouragement
expression
exportable
emission

### F f
formal
formulates

### G g

### H h
healthier

### I i
interactive      intervention
insignificant    inventor
irreplaceable    inspectors
independent      inject
independence     infectious
international    imperfectly
importance       indestructable
impossibility    incredible

### J j

### K k

### L l
leadership

### M m
magnetic
misplaced
misleading

### N n
national
nationalities

### O o
overweight       objections

### P p
powerful         portable
powerfully       predictions
powerless        permission
pleasures        prevention
pressurized      projectors
performance      perfectly

### Q q

### R r
recreation       repress
reactions        reformed
reappeared       reporters
resignation      retraction

### S s
signature        supervision
significant      subtraction
spectators

### T t
transaction      television
transportation   tractor
transmitted

### U u
underweight      unimpressive
uncovered        unpredictable
undercover       uninspired
unhealthiest

### V v

### W w

### X x        Y y        Z z

**Lesson 1**

t t s r h g b i e

**Lesson 2**

t s s r n h h g b i e

**Lesson 3**

t n m g c i e a

**Lesson 4**

z t n m g d i e e e a

# Reproducible Word Strips

**Lesson 6**  **Lesson 7**  **Lesson 8**  **Lesson 9**

| Lesson 6 | Lesson 7 | Lesson 8 | Lesson 9 |
|---|---|---|---|
| w | y | w | w |
| s | w | v | t |
| r | r | t | r |
| p | p | r | h |
| l | l | h | n |
| o | f | g | h |
| e | u | o | g |
| e | o | i | d |
|   | e | e | u |
|   |   | e | i |
|   |   |   | e |
|   |   |   | e |

CD-2420 Big Words for Big Kids

**Lesson 11**  **Lesson 12**  **Lesson 13**  **Lesson 14**

| Lesson 11 | Lesson 12 | Lesson 13 | Lesson 14 |
|---|---|---|---|
| t | t | s | s |
| s | r | s | s |
| r | n | r | p |
| r | n | p | l |
| c | c | l | d |
| u | o | u | d |
| e | i | e | i |
| e | e | e | e |
| a | e | e | e |
|   | a | a | a |

# Reproducible Word Strips

| Lesson 16 | Lesson 17 | Lesson 18 | Lesson 19 |
|---|---|---|---|
| a e e c r s s t | a e i o c n r s t | a e e i i c n r t t y | a a i o c n n r s t t |

**Lesson 21**     **Lesson 22**     **Lesson 23**     **Lesson 24**

Lesson 21: y v s r d c o i e

Lesson 22: v r r n d c u o e e

Lesson 23: r p p d e e a a a

Lesson 24: s r p p n d c i e e a a a

# Reproducible Word Strips

**Lesson 26**

r n n g g g c u n o u o i e a

**Lesson 27**

s r g p p p c u n o t i e a

**Lesson 28**

t r n n m g c u o e e e a

**Lesson 29**

y s r l g c n n u o o o e a

**Lesson 31**

a e i u g n r s t

**Lesson 32**

a e i i o g n n r s t

**Lesson 33**

a e i g m n n s s t

**Lesson 34**

a i i i i c f g n n n s t

# Reproducible Word Strips

**Lesson 36**   **Lesson 37**   **Lesson 38**   **Lesson 39**

Lesson 36: a e i c d l m p s

Lesson 37: a a e e e i b c l l p r r

Lesson 38: a e i i d g l m n s

Lesson 39: a e e i d h l p r r s

**Lesson 41**

t p n n n d d i e e e

**Lesson 42**

p n n n n d d c i e e e e

**Lesson 43**

t t n n n l o i i i e a a

**Lesson 44**

t t s n n l o i i i e a a

# Reproducible Word Strips

**Lesson 46**

a e e i h h l r t

**Lesson 47**

a a i i i o c c f l n s s t

**Lesson 48**

a a i i i o c c f l n s s t

**Lesson 49**

a e i c d f l s s y

**Lesson 51**

e e i d g n p r s

**Lesson 52**

e e i o n p r s s x

**Lesson 53**

e e i i u m n p r s s v

**Lesson 54**

e e i u d p r r s s z

# Reproducible Word Strips

| Lesson 56 | Lesson 57 | Lesson 58 | Lesson 59 |
|---|---|---|---|
| r | r | y | t |
| r | r | t | s |
| p | m | r | r |
| n | f | m | m |
| m | d | f | l |
| f | o | d | f |
| c | e | d | u |
| o | e | i | o |
| e | | e | e |
| e | | | e |
| a | | | a |

**Lesson 61**

e e o p r r r s t

**Lesson 62**

a e i o c m n p r t

**Lesson 63**

a a i o o n n p r r s t t t

**Lesson 64**

a e e o b l p r t x

# Reproducible Word Strips

**Lesson 66**

e i i o c d n p r s t

**Lesson 67**

a e e i u b c d l n p r t

**Lesson 68**

a i i o o c c d n n r s t t

**Lesson 69**

a i i o c d h p r s t t

CD-2420 Big Words for Big Kids

**Lesson 71**

e i i o m n p r s s

**Lesson 72**

a e i d m n r s t t t

**Lesson 73**

e o o c m p r s s

**Lesson 74**

i i i o b l m p s s t y

CD-2420 Big Words for Big Kids © Carson-Dellosa

| Lesson 76 | Lesson 77 | Lesson 78 | Lesson 79 |
|---|---|---|---|
| y t r p n o i e e | y t t r n n o i i e e | t s s r p n c o i e | t t s s r p c o e a |

CD-2420 Big Words for Big Kids

# Reproducible Word Strips

**Lesson 81**

e e i i o l n s t v

**Lesson 82**

e i i o u n p r s s v

**Lesson 83**

a i o u b c n r s t t

**Lesson 84**

a e i o c n r r t t

CD-2420 Big Words for Big Kids

# Reproducible Word Strips

**Lesson 86**

e o o c j p r r s t

**Lesson 87**

e i o o b c j n s t

**Lesson 88**

e i i u d n n p r r s

**Lesson 89**

a i o o c n p r r s s t

# Reproducible Word Strips

## Lesson 91
e i i o u c f n s t

## Lesson 92
e e i c f l m p r t y

## Lesson 93
i o o u c c n n r s t t

## Lesson 94
e e i i u b c d l n r s t t

CD-2420 Big Words for Big Kids

**Lesson 96**

i i o o b g l s s t

**Lesson 97**

a i i i o b c n s t t

**Lesson 98**

e e i i b c d l n r

**Lesson 99**

e i o c d r r s t

# References

Brown, L. (Ed.) (1993). *The New Shorter Oxford English Dictionary on Historical Principles.* Oxford (UK): Clarendon Press.